The
ONION COOKBOOK

JEAN BOTHWELL

The
ONION COOKBOOK

with illustrations by
MARGARET AYER

Dover Publications, Inc., New York

Published in Canada by General Publishing Com-
pany, Ltd., 30 Lesmill Road, Don Mills, Toronto,
Ontario.
Published in the United Kingdom by Constable
and Company, Ltd., 10 Orange Street, London
WC 2.

This Dover edition, first published in 1976, is an
unabridged and corrected republication of the work
originally published in 1950 under the title *Onions
without Tears*. It is reprinted by special arrange-
ment with the original publisher, Hastings House
Publisher, Inc., 10 East 40th Street, New York,
New York 10016. The information which appeared
on the endpapers in the original edition is repro-
duced on pages viii and ix of this edition.

International Standard Book Number: 0-486-23312-X
Library of Congress Catalog Card Number: 75-35403

Manufactured in the United States of America
Dover Publications, Inc.
180 Varick Street
New York, N.Y. 10014

ONIONS

Come, follow me by the smell,
Here are delicate onions to sell;
I promise to use you well.
They make the blood warmer,
You'll feed like a farmer;
For this is every cook's opinion,
No savoury dish without an onion;
But, lest your kissing should be spoiled,
Your onions must be thoroughly boiled:
    Or else you may spare
    Your mistress a share,
The secret will never be known:
    She cannot discover
    The breath of her lover,
But think it as sweet as her own.

From *Verses for Fruitwomen*
JONATHAN SWIFT
(1667–1745)

Contents

STANDARD MEASUREMENTS
AND ABBREVIATIONS

tsp.   — teaspoon   1 saltspoon — $\frac{1}{4}$ tsp.
tbsp. — tablespoon   3 tsp. — 1 tbsp.
q.s.   — quantity sufficient   16 tbsp. — 1 cup
lb.   — pound   1 cup — 8 oz.
oz.   — ounce   2 cups — 1 pint

All spoon measurements, rounded
All cup measurements level,
unless otherwise indicated

CANNED FRUITS AND VEGETABLES

#1 can — 1-1/3 cups
#2 can — $2\frac{1}{2}$ cups
#$2\frac{1}{2}$ can — $3\frac{1}{2}$ cups
#3 can — 4 cups
1 can soup — $10\frac{1}{2}$ oz.

THESE EACH EQUAL ONE POUND

2 cups liquid

2 cups granulated sugar

2½ cups brown sugar

4 cups all purpose flour

5 cups cake flour

2 cups grated cheese

2½ cups vegetable shortening

2 cups butter

MISCELLANEOUS

2 slices soft bread make
1 cup cubes

½ a large Bermuda onion
equals 1 cup chopped, or

2 medium-sized white onions make
1 cup, chopped

CONVERSION TABLES FOR FOREIGN EQUIVALENTS

DRY INGREDIENTS

Ounces	Grams	Grams	Ounces	Pounds	Kilograms	Kilograms	Pounds
1 =	28.35	1 =	0.035	1 =	0.454	1 =	2.205
2	56.70	2	0.07	2	0.91	2	4.41
3	85.05	3	0.11	3	1.36	3	6.61
4	113.40	4	0.14	4	1.81	4	8.82
5	141.75	5	0.18	5	2.27	5	11.02
6	170.10	6	0.21	6	2.72	6	13.23
7	198.45	7	0.25	7	3.18	7	15.43
8	226.80	8	0.28	8	3.63	8	17.64
9	255.15	9	0.32	9	4.08	9	19.84
10	283.50	10	0.35	10	4.54	10	22.05
11	311.85	11	0.39	11	4.99	11	24.26
12	340.20	12	0.42	12	5.44	12	26.46
13	368.55	13	0.46	13	5.90	13	28.67
14	396.90	14	0.49	14	6.35	14	30.87
15	425.25	15	0.53	15	6.81	15	33.08
16	453.60	16	0.57				

LIQUID INGREDIENTS

Liquid Ounces	Milliliters	Milliliters	Liquid Ounces	Quarts	Liters	Liters	Quarts
1 =	29.573	1 =	0.034	1 =	0.946	1 =	1.057
2	59.15	2	0.07	2	1.89	2	2.11
3	88.72	3	0.10	3	2.84	3	3.17
4	118.30	4	0.14	4	3.79	4	4.23
5	147.87	5	0.17	5	4.73	5	5.28
6	177.44	6	0.20	6	5.68	6	6.34
7	207.02	7	0.24	7	6.62	7	7.40
8	236.59	8	0.27	8	7.57	8	8.45
9	266.16	9	0.30	9	8.52	9	9.51
10	295.73	10	0.33	10	9.47	10	10.57

Gallons (American)	Liters	Liters	Gallons (American)
1 =	3.785	1 =	0.264
2	7.57	2	0.53
3	11.36	3	0.79
4	15.14	4	1.06
5	18.93	5	1.32
6	22.71	6	1.59
7	26.50	7	1.85
8	30.28	8	2.11
9	34.07	9	2.38
10	37.86	10	2.74

Foreword

It could be that American cooks have taken longer than they should to realize the value and versatility of onions. Or perhaps they seem more important to me because I was denied them in childhood. It was only after I grew up and got a kitchen of my own that I fully realized what I had missed—the repeated fragrance of an onion and potato soup, steaming hot on a chilly day in fall; fried onions, sizzling with liver in a pan; and the creamy brown necklace round a pot roast.

I can remember the day, at the age of four, when I first met potato soup with onions in it, for lunch at my best friend's. Later, at home, when I demanded to know why we never had such a soup, I learned that my mother couldn't abide onions, neither taste nor smell. So began the long wait that ended eventually in a little galley of a kitchen where my collection of onion recipes could be translated into soup, salad, and baked, boiled, steamed, or fried onions, with impunity.

It has been wonderful, right up to the night when two friends came for dinner and I served my version of creamed onions with steak, and one of the guests said, "Mmmm! You ought to do a book." Those six words have become a part of speech where I live and they are not always meant to be taken literally. But I did, that time, and I offer here the brief I hold for the versatility of ONIONS.

What other vegetable, without too frequent repetition, can become hors d'oeuvres, soup, main dish, or auxiliary and general flavorer for every course of a meal except dessert? Even that, for one of the recipes recommended herein as a main motif of a luncheon or supper is a pie in form and structure. There is also a rich butternut pudding with a "very small onion cut very fine" in it, of shaker origin. And one of my friends who has lived in India a good few years insists that her cook serves onion-flavored ice cream when he gets his spoons mixed.

So, I offer you the onions I know and they may suggest others to those researchers who find these pages good.

The
ONION COOKBOOK

Quantity Sufficient For Four
In Every Recipe
Unless Otherwise Indicated

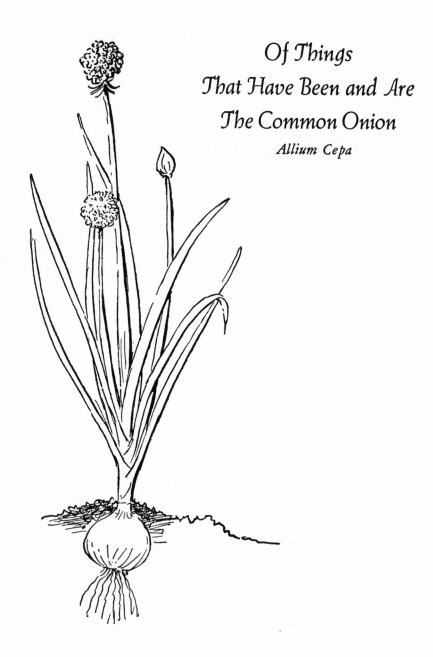

CHAPTER 1

Of Things
That Have Been and Are
The Common Onion
Allium Cepa

ONIONS belong to the lily family, the *alliums,* a great company of flower and vegetable, gracing rock gardens and providing modern man with concentrated vitamins and mineral food in their succulent bulbs.

The wilds of Asia are believed to be the home of the first onion, a thin flat reed of a thing, practically all neck, and little like its firm-fleshed descendant under cultivation as a national industry in the United States and a staple crop in several other countries.

It's a long, long way from the hinterlands of Asia to present-day farms and markets in the United States, but the onion was a great traveler and a great leveler too. Its name comes from the Latin, *unio,* the philologists say, meaning unity, many things in one. And all men have thirst and hunger and health in common. So, because it was early found to be a thirst preventive, and because it was a food, either fresh or dried, and because it had inherent medicinal properties, it was brought out of the remoteness of the east in the saddlebags of caravans, riding with a conqueror, or in his servant's turban, spreading, multiplying, rewarding, as civilization crept westward.

In the early days of discovery and settlement in the North American continent, sailors coming off ships after their long voyages without grace of greens, were delighted to find wild onions growing in the New World and "garliks" for their "salats."

Many of these indigenous varieties have been domesticated and developed here by commercial growers and seedsmen just as European gardeners adapted the first Asiatic traveler and made it into the Italian and Spanish and Egyptian onions known in world markets now. The new onions are milder, larger, firmer, more manageable and enjoyable and they are available in several strengths the year round so that cooks have a choice of kind for the recipe of the day.

As a result a fragrance has begun to blow a little more steadily across the land, from Trader Vic's in San Francisco along the Harvey route, and via the ranges and ovens of the Middle West, all the way to Mulberry Street on the lower East Side of New York.

They fry the lily on Mulberry Street, with peppers and sausage in a big pan on a pushcart during the feast of San Gennaro and they serve the mixture in huge cuts of Italian bread that stretch your mouth. Seasoned with the joy of festival and eaten under the sharp light of the great arches of electricity above, it is the best sandwich in the world. Everyone else is chewing too and where everybody eats them nobody fusses about the smell, not that kind of smell. It can't be compared to anything except itself, and it's wonderful.

It is the Bermuda they fry and the big Spanish, larger than a woman's fist. The thick creamy slices are piled, ready for the pan, and huge peeled globes mounded, ready for the slicing. They have a light of their own, with the red of tomatoes and big green peppers. The stalls do not need any other decoration. One cart after another, they line the curb on both sides of the street right down to the saint's altar at the end.

Onions and sausage and light and crowds! And it seems a long time, after the last sandwich, on the last night of the feast, to wait until next year for another. They don't taste the same anywhere else. Not even out of one's own kitchen.

It's the same way with the French fried ones, down in Louisiana at that famous place on False River. After you've eaten those they don't taste the same anywhere else, either. Maybe it's the hunger one brings in after the long drive to get there. But you get hungry at home.

Out in the Middle West, in a former home town of mine, there was Aquila Court, famed in its own area for its food and for its association with much that was good and distinguished there. It had many specialities—mushroom soup, chicken salad julienne served in green-pointed glass bowls, and the first and finest coffee ice cream—but only one of the list has a place here, the *Scallop of Onions* offered to every luncheoner, when he had ordered and his service had come, in much the same way that baked beans turn up at one's elbow in Boston as an adjunct to the menu of the day. That *Scallop*! Just talking about it, one sees again the fountain in the Court, the grey stone flags of the floor, the delicate green of the decor; and the golden look of the dish comes back to mind and the marvellous smell. I think it had nutmeg in it.

It is good for every one to take a gustatory journey once in a while, if only in the mind. It renews appreciation and gives a fillip to routine, even though in retrospect food that once seemed fit for the gods is proved simple rather than mysterious and not difficult to reproduce. And onions go with many things, one finds, and anywhere, from red-checked tablecloths and the light of an oil wick, to smooth damask and shining candelabra. The taste and the flavor are the same, if they are right.

Balzac liked onions well enough to eat them for breakfast, lunch, and dinner. There was no food more propitious to the mind, he maintained, "rendering it subtle and putting to flight base notions and prejudices."

In this gathering of the ways of an onion on a stove and with a cook, I have omitted Balzac's breakfasts. But there are recipes for every other meal of the day—simply and easily prepared, only a few with frills—and some general rules that govern the use of onions in any dish, to prove in their entirety and all over again that Balzac was right.

CHAPTER 2

Fundamentals of Onion Cooking

The rose of roots

ROBERT LOUIS STEVENSON

The worth of onions as a food has been steadily increasing in recent decades in the United States. Gardeners, with much patience and a long view, have improved seeds, crossing breeds to make a milder onion, and have adapted it to cultivation in the many different climate regions of our country so ably that there isn't a season when some variety is not in the market. In a good crop year its price is reasonable enough to be included in even the strictest budgeting. It has medicinal properties of real value in special diets and is a general stimulant to digestion.

For all these reasons the onion could and should be on every American table, but it is still neglected by many cooks. The explanation, beyond taste and odor prejudice, is difficult for an onionophile to understand. He argues that inasmuch as there is nothing wrong, not anything really, with an onion, the fault must lie with the cooks. It is they who do not understand, finally.

My own feeling is that anything made with onions can be better and richer if the cook selects the right onion in the right season. Because most of us have been taking those that are handiest or the kind the grocer wants us to buy, results have not been perfect and the cook blames the vegetable. So, as a means to the desired understanding and to promote an acquaintance that may ripen into friendship, these few discoveries and principles of onion cooking are offered here. Some attempt has been made to suggest the right variety for a particular dish. But many kinds

7

are known only in the region where they are cultivated, so no differentiation is given except sweet white, Spanish red or yellow, and Bermuda, for the most part.

There are several classifications, however, into which all onions easily fall: (a) a color division—red, yellow and white; (b) usage—raw, best for boiling, salads, pickles, etc.; (c) the imports, Italian and Spanish, and the so-called natives, the American varieties which have been developed from these.

Prize Taker is a popular American onion, growing to a great size in a cool, moist locality. This is a mild onion with pure crisp white flesh under its thin yellow skin. It can easily be mistaken for a Spanish variety.

Chives and scallions are for fresh use. The big sweet Bermudas and Southports are for drying and storing for winter. White Bunching produces the little pearls for pickling.

Shallots (*Allium Ascalonicum*). Ascalon is a seaport in Palestine, associated with the Crusades, and the derived French form of the word for the onion from Ascalon, *eschaloigne,* becomes our English one, *scallion.* This confusion of science and speech has probably given rise to the belief by many cooks that baby onions and shallots are the same, which they definitely are not.

The true shallot has a milder flavor than an onion, yet it is so distinctive that like garlic, a little is enough. This is the reason that chefs constantly indicate shallots in their recipes. It is the onion of the epicure, ideal for sauces and delicate blendings, but not best for stews where a more vigorous and pronounced flavor is required. It is fine for seasoning poultry.

Shallots are never marketed in the green state except for use as a substitute for scallions. Look for small dry rose-pink bulbs, quite uniform in size. They are sometimes called potato onions or multipliers, for the reason that the little bulbs grow in a cluster and each section in the cluster is like a small onion set. If planted in the spring in the same way ordinary onion sets are used, each one will subdivide instead of increasing the size of the single bulb. If served as spring onions are, cleaned and raw, three or four plants will be enough for a meal.

Webster says that a *scallion* is "any onion forming a thick basal portion without a bulb." The same may be said of a leek. So the difference here is, essentially, that scallions are grown for table use immediately from the garden, and are generally eaten raw, while a leek is always cooked.

If one is a purchaser and not a gardener there are still characteristics of the onion worth knowing. Don't buy those that have begun to sprout, or the ones that have a thick, soft neck, or that feel spongy in the bulb. Buy firm hard onions, with tight thin necks and crisp covering skin, whether bronze or yellow or white.

Store home supplies in a cool dry place. If space is limited buy only a few at a time, but try to keep on hand always, a supply of the small sweet white ones, or a mild medium sized Spanish. The most careful planning doesn't allow for that emergency when you need to change a meal all round in a hurry. And sometimes just one onion is an enormous help.

It rained one night and we couldn't go out for dinner, as planned. But I had some cold roast beef, a part of a green pepper, some mushrooms and one sweet big Bermuda onion. I used half of it and all the rest of the makings and produced something that by no rule of thumb or spoon could be repeated but it disappeared and we were a little glad it had rained. That is what I mean by keeping an onion in the house. Onion or doctor, a need is met.

CALENDAR

April to July—Onions from Egypt and Chile are available in American markets. Also several Bermuda and Spanish varieties come north from Texas, which has become an extensive onion-producing section.

From August to the following spring, the stronger American varieties are to be found.

October to June—The sweet Spanish grown in the Northwest come to the eastern markets.

Round the year one has the small yellow Spanish.

Some regional varieties are not easily shipped far. This is particularly true of the red ones grown in California.

Add to everything the supplies in private households from the small gardens grown in back yards and vacant lots, and then one has a more complete picture of America's sources for onions. In a good year the annual crop of this country alone amounts to more than seven million bushels, and the figure is on the increase. One might wonder why it has seemed necessary to urge greater consumption. Perhaps there is a Samaritan element in it—a desire to show others what they are missing.

PROPERTIES OF THE ONION

As a Food   Our grandmothers understood that some kinds of food could do more for health and growth than others, without knowing how or why. Now we know that the chemical compounds in vegetables and cereals and milk and eggs contribute specific aids to good living. These chemicals are called vitamins and in their various combinations have been isolated by laboratory tests so that sources are certain.

It is clear now why the onion has always been regarded as a health-giving vegetable—that it was good aside from its flavor, because it made one sleep. It has been the vitamins all the time, B and G, and C, particularly C. In New York, onion soup has been promoted to first place as a nightcap in supper clubs. They still think it makes them sleep.

In addition, the onion has a large amount of protein, mineral salt, nitrogen, starch and uncrystallized sugar. Even the tops are worth drying for use; chemical analysis has found calcium and nitrogen concentrated there.

It is the volatile oil in onions, rich in sulphur, which gives them their pungent smell and taste. Boiling removes the oily content more than any other method of cooking. But it is a chemical property, a lachrymator isolated by chemists, which is known to cause the tears, a substance akin to the tear gases manufactured commercially.

Because of the oil and the sugar there are 125 calories in a medium sized onion. The calorie-counter must always make choices, so, knowing their value in the day's quota, it should be no hardship to give onions a place even in a reducing diet.

As a Medicine   An old cook book, dating back to 1859, advises one to take the heart out of a roasted onion and slip it into the ear "as warm as can be borne," at the same time soaking the feet in hot water. Having read this primitive method of curing earache one realizes what a far road we have come in medical thought as well as in the growth of onions. The therapeutic value of this remedy lay in the ability of the onion heart to hold heat, no doubt, and the patient's thought of warmth and comfort did the rest.

There was also an onion syrup for colds and a poultice to be tied on the hands and feet of infants too small to take the cough mixture.

These old ideas have a place here to round out my premise, i.e., the value of the onion to mankind. Our grandmothers did with what they had and raised no less sturdy families.

COOKING METHODS

Always peel dried onions from the root and toward the top. A thin slice will sever the small rootlets and release the first and second layers of the bulb. If they are not too dry, or haven't begun to wither from storage in a warm place, the silvery or bronze brown paper-thin sheath of the bulb is all you will have to remove. But if you are doubtful, take the next layer off too, until you reach the first moisture. There is a protective thin covering for each layer of the bulb, which slips off easily when moist. It will only spoil the finished dish if a tough, resistant-to-heat layer gets in.

Consider the recipe and choose for it the most adaptable onion out of those available:

1. Red Spanish are best for baking. There is so much steam in the oven from the natural moisture that a mild onion would be almost flavorless when done.

2. White mild onions are best to use raw in salads. The sweet purple Italian onion is also good for this purpose, and it adds an unusual color note as well.

3. Yellow Spanish are a good choice to bake stuffed. So are large Bermudas. Size is also important for baking, particularly for use as a main dish, so that the shell holding the stuffing may be firm and still leave room enough for a good serving of the center mixture.

4. Use small white sweet onions for creaming or for cream soups.

BOILED ONIONS   Choose small or medium-sized onions to boil whole. Larger ones are better sliced if they are to be boiled before creaming, or parboiled for frying. Slice the large ones first, then peel. The tough outer ring will slip off easily and save you time. With a sharp knife make a cross-cut in the top of each onion to be boiled whole. This will prevent the centers coming out, as the moisture inside swells the onion during cooking.

Lemon juice or a dash of vinegar in the water will help preserve the whiteness of onions. If cooked too long they will turn dark. This can happen, too, if there is not enough water in the pan.

If onions are old, start them cooking in cold water. They need a little longer to cook, softening gradually, as the water heats. Old onions are stronger-flavored than new, no matter what their variety.

All young vegetables should be started in boiling salted water and covered tightly while cooking.

If you are obliged to boil an extra strong onion, a red one, perhaps, cook in an uncovered kettle in enough boiling water to cover. Add salt, one tablespoon to a quart of water.

If there is water left when the boil is done, drain and keep as stock for a soup base. Such a stock will keep in the refrigerator and can be used for clear soup or a creamed one, with a left-over gravy for thickening, as an expedient, and for variety of flavor. Make in proportion of three cups onion liquid to one cup milk. If you have no white sauce on hand, one tablespoon of butter and one of flour, with seasoning, to each cup of liquid for the soup is the proportion for a thin cream soup. Allow for steak gravy and reduce the amount of other liquid if that is to be used.

It is a fuel saver to boil onions in the oven. Use an earthenware baking dish and barely cover the onions with boiling salted water. This method is held to improve the flavor.

The oil in onions is reduced by boiling more than by any other way of cooking them. On account of the marked oil content, use scant measurements of butter for the roux when creaming onions.

BAKED OR ROASTED ONIONS When roasting onions with other vegetables around a pot roast, put the onions in first, at least a half hour ahead of potatoes and carrots. They require longer cooking than most vegetables do, and should be almost transparent in the outer layers when done.

Onions can be successfully baked by themselves, in their skins as potatoes are, because they have enough moisture to create steam within. See Chapter 4.

FRIED AND SAUTÉED ONIONS   The principles of any French frying pertain to onions. Recipes will be found in Chapter 4.

Don't serve these crisp onions on the same plate with juicy meat or other moist foods. The onions will absorb the liquid and lose their shape. And don't cover them up if there is a small delay after cooking. They'll go limp as wet paper.

Sautéing is a form of frying, distinguished from *frying* by the method. To sauté onions, they should be done slowly over even heat and constantly turned so that they will cook but not brown. Sautéed onions are used a great deal in making sauces or in the preliminary step for a dish in which onions are not a main ingredient but merely a seasoning aid.

ONIONS IN SALAD

Raw onions are difficult for some people to digest yet the raw state seems most desirable in salad. Here is an alternative. Peel and slice a large Spanish or Bermuda onion, cover with boiling water and let stand for a half hour. Drain, cover with the same amount of ice cold water and leave another half hour to crisp. Drain again and combine with other salad ingredients or serve alone with desired dressing.

COLOR NOTE

Now that the onion is seen in all the best places, it should look its best. Many dishes with an onion base are too pallid and therefore lose appeal. Dust a cream soup or a bowl of creamed onions with paprika or a pinch of black pepper—pepper goes with onions as the salt in the ocean. Minced parsley helps too, even when the recipe doesn't call for it, and the yellow drift of grated cheese along with the paprika is a thought to pursue. You'll have some of your own, no doubt. Reference is made to this need in the chapter on chives. Taste depends a lot on vision.

ONIONS AS A SEASONING

MINCED ONION   Peel the onion as for cooking. Cut in half. Hold one of the halves in your hand and slash it with a knife in minute crisscrosses. Scrape the resulting mince into a bowl and repeat until you have the amount necessary for the recipe.

ONION JUICE   Bottled onion juice loses its strength so it is better to prepare it freshly at the time of using. Cut a slice from the bottom or root end of an onion that is large enough to hold comfortably in the hand and twist on the grater as one does any fruit that is being juiced. A small plastic grater designed for this purpose is ideal, as it does not retain the odor. A fruit press may be used if it is the sort that will not taint the next fruit juice you squeeze.

In flavoring with the pure juice of an onion do not add until the dish is almost ready to serve. High heat will destroy the flavor on account of the oil content. This is a good seasoning to add to creamed potatoes or to the mixture for mashed potato cakes.

WITH A CASSEROLE   For flavoring a baked dish that does not include onions necessarily, rub the sides and bottom with a fresh-cut piece, as one does a salad bowl with garlic, before pouring in the ingredients for the baking.

ONION SALT   There are a number of commercially prepared brands of onion salt and dried flakes of onion on the market. The salt is really a dehydrated form of onion with corn starch added to prevent caking. One teaspoon of onion salt is the equivalent in flavor value of one fresh onion. Unless one uses a great deal of this preparation, it is well to remember that it loses strength after opening and if let stay on the shelf too long the amount used now and then will have to be adjusted to time and the recipe. There is also a danger that too much at any time will produce a bitter instead of a pleasant taste. The chief convenience of the salt form is for seasoning when there isn't time to use a fresh onion, with the cosmetic routine attached.

ONION FLAKES   These seem to keep their strength better than the salt. A handful dropped in the water in which string beans or peas are cooking adds much to the flavor of the dish. Toss a couple of teaspoonsful into the kettle when preparing plain boiled potatoes. Besides pointing up their flavor, the seasoned water is a good potential for soup stock.

SEASONING ONIONS THEMSELVES

Onions and pepper, black, fine pepper, seem to have an affinity. There is also nutmeg for creamed ones, with paprika sprinkled on top, or parsley chopped fine, for the color and the added piquancy. And an occasional clove. Plus mustard. And dill.

Remember that it makes a difference if you are seasoning a hot or a cold dish. The cold takes more salt.

STORING A CUT ONION

If it is necessary to put away a part of a cut onion, store it in a glass container that has a glass lid or one with a plastic lid. A metal top will retain the odor where glass will not. It seems a little superfluous to include a warning to cover anything in this modern day of ice-box containers designed for every conceivable need. But onions and garlic are generous with their flavor, especially to milk and cream. If the cream has been meant for dessert peaches or the chocolate pudding, the gift isn't as appreciated as it might be, even though this book is all on the side of the angels—onion angels.

QUANTITIES

Use one pound of onions for four people, if the dish is part of a dinner course. If it be the main dish of the meal, allow at least three medium sized onions per person, or one large Bermuda, if stuffed. The number in a pound varies of course with the size of the onion. For two people cook from one-half to two-thirds of a pound. Quantity depends somewhat too on the state of the onion itself, and how much of the outer layer of each bulb has to be discarded. Unless otherwise indicated, the amounts in all recipes in this book are meant to serve four people.

COOKING TIME

To boil small white onions, allow about 25 minutes. Larger, medium sized yellow ones take longer. At the half hour they should be very nearly done. It is best to slice for boiling any onion larger than the small white ones. A saucepan full of sliced ones should not take more than 15 minutes when the water is again brought to the boiling point after adding the onions.

For baking allow about half an hour in a moderate oven for onion cases that have been parboiled and the stuffiing precooked. Otherwise, test tender with a silver fork.

UTENSILS

There are probably as many theories as there are cooks about the best utensils for cooking onions. I prefer glass or earthenware for baking them and an iron skillet for creaming or frying. If any of the heavy sheet metal kettles are used, they should be scoured immediately afterward, as the sulphur content in the onion turns them black, and taste does cling a little. The bottom part of a glass double-boiler or an enamel kettle, if the surface is not cracked or chipped, are the best for boiling.

I keep one special paring knife to use with onions. It has a green handle—a go-ahead in more than one way.

ODOR

Failing a commercial preparation for subduing all cooking odors in a small house, a little vinegar put on the stove in an uncovered pan during cooking will keep the smell of boiling onions from becoming offensive.

COSMETIC NOTES

Among the many things that Benjamin Franklin is known to have said and those attributed which he did not, is a remark that "Onions can make even heirs and widows weep." But nowadays they must look elsewhere for a starter of their crocodile tears. Chemists are cooperating with Experiment Farms and the lachrymator element in onions is being worked upon. Meantime, these suggestions are offered for immediate help to prevent tears while peeling.

1. Heat small onions before peeling and you will not weep.
2. Peel under spray from cold water tap.
3. Or, while peeling, hold a toothpick in your mouth, unless you prefer a crust of bread.

The argument about these various methods never abates. The main thing is to get the onions peeled, if you or the family like them well enough to take the tear hurdle. I belong to the under-water school, even though I think at the same time that having an onion in the stew is worth weeping for.

To remove onion odor from the hands, rinse under cold water, rub hard with salt, or freshly chopped parsley, or celery tops, or lemon, and then wash with soap and cold water.

For the breath, eat a little sugar, or chew a coffee bean, or a sprig of fresh parsley, or a clove. Drink some strong black coffee, or a glass of milk.

Manufacturers have gone into the matter of tainted breath seriously and there is now on the market an aromatic liquid that will do in a moment what one has heretofore accomplished more tediously with the parsley treatment.

There is also a tear reducer in the form of a clever little covered chopper that is guaranteed to turn out the proper degree of mince or pulp for the recipe of the moment, and no harm done to vision.

And there is promise of a toothpaste to come that will combine the qualities of cleanser and deodorant in one, with onions and garlic particularly in mind.

CHAPTER 3

In Soups

The juice of leeks and onions,
  Who fondly sips,
    To kiss the fair
Must close his lips.

ANON.

Soup *du jour*—of any day and any meal—the main dish for lunch, in winter; the appetite teaser before the roast at dinner; the post-midnight snack, outmoding scrambled eggs; ONION SOUP, *messieurs* and *mesdames,* in these several guises, with or without a flavor collaborator.

The making of a soup may begin with a *roux,* the first step for a cream soup. It may begin with the soup bone brought from the butcher for vegetable soup. Its base may be only the can lifted from the pantry shelf, a clear consommé to which one adds a bit of sliced lemon and minced parsley and onion salt. If any soup has an onion in it, it is royal of its kind, and if it is served the day after its making, when all the flavors have become one—then it is at its royal best. An ancient Scottish recipe called for oatmeal and a few marigold heads, but there were onions in it, too, and that was two hundred years ago.

COUSIN BELL'S CREAM OF ONION SOUP

3 medium sized Spanish onions
2 tbsp. butter
1 level tsp. flour
2 tbsp. bread crumbs
white pepper }
salt   } q.s.
2 cups milk

21

Melt the butter in a skillet and add the onions, sliced very thin. Brown slowly and lightly. Stir in the flour and bread crumbs, mixed with the seasoning. When fat and dry ingredients are well blended, add the milk slowly. It may be cold, but it is less likely to form lumps if the milk has been scalded beforehand. Remove to double boiler and cook one half hour. Sprinkle with paprika and serve.

THICK ONION SOUP

6 large yellow (Spanish) onions
3 tbsp. butter
1 tbsp. flour
4 medium sized potatoes
1 cup green peas (canned or fresh cooked)
1 cup light cream
pepper and salt, q.s.
pinch curry powder

Peel and chop the onions and sauté to light brown in the butter. Dust on the flour and blend. Add the potatoes which have been peeled and cubed, and enough water to cover. Simmer until tender and water is absorbed. Sieve onions, potatoes, and peas and thin the resulting purée with light cream to soup consistency. Heat through, but do not boil.

Serve with chopped fresh parsley, paprika or chopped chives garnish.

ANN'S GRANDMOTHER'S POTATO SOUP

3 medium sized potatoes
1 large Bermuda onion
1 egg
½ cup sour cream
¼ tsp. salt
5 cups water
4 level tsp. flour

Peel potatoes and cut in small cubes. Peel and mince the onion.

Put potatoes and onion in kettle together with 3 cups of water and cook until potatoes are soft and most of the water absorbed. Add half the salt.

Beat the egg thoroughly and mix with rest of the salt and the flour, to make a dough. Add the two remaining cups of water to the potato and onion mixture, bring to a boil, and drop the egg dough by bits into the soup. Dip the end of the spoon into the soup to do this. The drops must be about the size of a pea. They do not keep their shape.

Cook for about ten minutes, then remove from the fire and when boiling has stopped, add the sour cream. If the soup is still too thick, a little more water can be added before heating it through again to serve.

CREAM OF ONION SOUP WITH CHEESE
#1

    4 medium sized Spanish onions or 6 small white
    2 tbsp. butter
    2 tbsp. flour
    4 cups milk
    1 cup sharp cheese, grated or cut into small pieces
       pinch pepper, white or black
    ⅛ tsp. salt

Scald milk while peeling and dicing the onions fine.

Melt the butter in the soup kettle and toss the onions in it until they are browned. Dust with flour and blend. Pour on the warm milk, a little at a time, stirring constantly, until the mixture is smooth. Add cheese and stir until it has melted. Serve with pilot crackers.

#2

    5 medium size white onions
    3 tbsp. butter
    3 tbsp. flour
    4 cups milk
       salt and pepper, q.s.
    4 tbsp. grated Parmesan cheese

Peel onions and slice thin. Sauté in butter in top part of double boiler until lightly browned. Add flour and salt gradually, then the milk, stirring until smooth. Cook over the boiling water for 15 minutes more. It should be creamy and slightly thick when served. Sprinkle 1 tablespoonful of cheese over each cup.

ONION SOUP WITH CONSOMMÉ

1 lb. yellow onions
3 tbsp. butter
1 tbsp. flour
2 cups scalded milk
3 cups consommé (canned may be used)
   yolk of one egg
   season to taste

Peel and chop onions and cook in two tbsp. butter for ten minutes. Do not brown. Add consommé and cook about twenty minutes longer, or until onions are tender. Press through a sieve and set purée aside.

Make a *roux* from remaining butter and the flour. Blend in the warm milk and seasonings, stirring until the sauce is smooth. Add the sieved onions. Beat the egg slightly, add some of the hot stock gradually, and then combine with the rest of the soup. Bring just to boil and serve.

CREAM OF ONION SOUP WITH GREEN PEPPER

2 large Bermuda onions
4 tbsp. butter
3 tbsp. flour
4 cups soup stock (can be made with concentrate cubes)
1 tbsp. chopped green pepper
1 cup light cream
   seasonings q.s. as preferred

Sauté the onion in half the butter until tender.
Make a *roux* of 2 tbsp. butter and the flour, and blend in the

soup stock, until the mixture is smooth. Combine with onions and the chopped pepper, and cook until it bubbles. Add the heated cream and serve. Top each serving with a parsley leaf or a dusting of paprika or both.

For a smooth soup with no pieces of onion or pepper appearing strain the mixture through a coarse sieve before adding the cream.

CREAM OF PEA SOUP
(chilled)

1 can condensed pea soup

or

½ can each of pea and asparagus soup
1 can cold milk
  pinch of black pepper
  pinch of curry powder
½ tsp. Onion Salt
  pinch of paprika
½ carton whipping cream

Blend soup and seasonings and gradually add milk until smooth. Heat through but do not boil. Pour in a quart jar and store in refrigerator until ready to serve.

Garnish: Rub a bowl with a cut clove of garlic and whip the cream in it. Or mince half of a small sweet onion and fold into the cream after it is whipped. Let stand about a half hour before serving to allow the flavor to dominate the cream. Serve soup with a spoonful of cream on top, dusted with paprika.

DON'T save any of the seasoned cream to use tomorrow. It will be bitter and you will be sorry.

ONION CHOWDER

2 strips lean bacon, diced
2 cups chopped yellow onions
2 cups water
3 medium sized potatoes, diced
2 cups milk
½ cup cream

2½ tsp. salt
¼ tsp. pepper
1 tbsp. flour
1 tbsp. butter

Fry bacon in deep saucepan or kettle until brown. Add onions and sauté, removing the bacon before it gets too dark. Add potatoes and water, cook until tender and restore bacon to mixture.
Add milk, cream, and seasonings.

Make a *roux* of the flour and butter, thin with a little of the heated milk, and stir into the soup. Cook ten minutes, stirring constantly.

LITTLE ONION SOUP

2 bunches scallions
6 medium sized fresh mushrooms
1 tbsp. butter
1 tbsp. minced pimiento
1 tbsp. chopped parsley
½ tsp. salt
½ clove garlic
2 cups thin white sauce
2 cups water
½ cup coffee cream
1 egg yolk

Clean scallions (cut away roots and tips and prepare as for serving raw); chop in short lengths and cook until tender in the boiling salted water—about 15 minutes.

Melt butter, flavor with garlic, and remove clove.

Chop mushrooms which have been washed and peeled and sautéed in butter. Add parsley and combine with white sauce, scallions and remaining cooking water. Check seasoning and fold in the minced pimiento.

Bring mixture just to boil and add the cream into which the egg yolk has been beaten.

Garnish each cup and serve.

TOMATO AND ONION SOUP

2 medium sized Bermuda onions
3 tbsp. butter
1 can consommé
1 can tomato soup
1 cup water
1¼ cups milk
½ tsp. condiment sauce
½ tsp. sugar
⅛ tsp. salt

Slice the onions and sauté in butter until clear. Add consommé and water, cover, and cook 15 to 20 minutes, or until onions test tender with a silver fork.

Meantime blend tomato soup, cold milk, and seasonings and combine with first mixture. Bring just to boil and serve.

SQUASH AND ONION SOUP
(chilled)

1 good sized long yellow summer squash
2 Spanish onions or 1 large Bermuda
3 tbsp. butter
½ can clear chicken broth
1 cup coffee cream
⅛ tsp. paprika

Peel the squash and the onions and cut fine. Simmer in the butter over low heat until they are clear but not brown. Add broth and cook until tender. Sieve and check seasoning. Cool, add cream and chill before serving. Garnish: black pepper and chopped parsley.

"LOBSCOUSE"

This dish and its name are so old that no one seems to know the origin of either, though the recipe was brought to the United States from Manchester, England.

Peel and slice 6 medium sized potatoes and 2 medium sized onions (Spanish yellow); put on in 4½ cups of cold water and boil down to a pulpy mush; season with salt and pepper before taking off the fire. Add 2 tablespoons butter and stir before serving.

ONION SOUP WITH MASHED POTATOES

>   2 Bermuda onions
>   3 tbsp. tried-out fat from beef roast
>   3 tbsp. flour
>   2 cups boiling water
>   2½ cups cold mashed potato (2 large or 3 smaller potatoes).
>   4 cups milk
>   1 tbsp. freshly minced parsley

Peel and slice onions. Sauté in the fat. When tender, blend with the flour and add the boiling water slowly, stirring until the mixture begins to thicken. Scald the milk and combine with the mashed potato, beating to a creamy consistency, then add to onions in the skillet. Season. Strain into the tureen from which the soup will be served.

Garnish: Chopped chives

ONION MARMITE SOUP

Marmite was originally the French name for the round kettle or cooking pot in which soup was made. It is association that has transferred the term to the soup itself—what we know as bouillon, the essence of boiled beef, or *petite marmite*. This is the base of the soup known as French onion in most American restaurants.

>   3 Spanish onions
>   2 tbsp. butter
>   4 cups water
>   3 tsp. any good marmite or soup concentrate
>   salt and pepper, q.s.
>   4 slices hard toast—melba toast is good
>   ½ cup dry grated cheese

Dissolve the soup concentrate in ¼ cup of water. Peel the onions and slice thin. Sauté in the butter, stirring until only slightly brown. Add the 4 cups of water and when it is hot, pour in the dissolved soup concentrate, simmer until well blended, and season to taste. Do this cautiously because some soup cubes are quite salty.

Serve in individual French soup casseroles, the kind with a lid. Cut a round of toast to fit the top and float it there. Sprinkle the cheese on top of each and serve.

This soup can be made from meat stock, from the beginning, if one prefers.

SOUPE A L'OIGNON

In France, in the country and the tucked-away restaurants in the cities, onion soup is another matter. Onions, sliced and browned in butter until well done, to which hot water is added and the whole seasoned and allowed to simmer down is the real *soupe a l'oignon,* although they do sometimes add a poultry or beef stock.

If the full history of the old Parker House in Boston is ever written, among its many contributions to the American cuisine will be onion soup, high on the list. The old chef who made it famous thought his secret would die with him. But he reckoned without the inquisitive twelve-year-old who had an early yen to cook and who watched every move when she was allowed in his kitchen.

Her soup is now a conversation piece at table or away from it. The kettle in which it is always done was the reward of long search in second-hand byways and now is more precious than the family jewels. Her husband's assignments at one time led them from Maine to California and the onion kettle went along with the hand luggage, where it could be watched—a possession fully as important as the baby's formula and the extra socks and toothbrushes.

The recipe? It was not offered me and I didn't ask. But I gathered that the sliced onions give of their essence after a day-long brew in layers in that heavy, tight-lidded kettle after which they become ambrosia for gods and men.

AUTUMN SOUP

This is one of the immeasurables. Its limits are a family's size and appetite and the content of an end-of-the-summer garden. It has a more homely flavor for me than other soups because mine has always a homemade condiment—nostalgia.

Everybody begins with a soup bone to make this recipe. It's beef at my house. And there are never any turnips in the soup. They're too aggressive somehow—they can outdo an onion any day in subduing other flavors (if there is too much onion, I mean). But after ruling out turnips, everything else is welcome. Green cabbage, shredded; carrots, the vigor of red onions, the small potatoes left in a hill, tomatoes; and all of it seasoned to taste and with hunger.

It is made best when the harvest moon is at the full and just before the first frost. The bell peppers are still plump and crisp and showing faintly red among their thick leaves. Cabbage snaps off its stem with a loud plunk. The field mice are beginning to rustle round in the cornstalk tents for a winter roof. The days are growing so cool that an applewood fire has a pleasant crackle in the evening. That's the ideal time for vegetable soup, plates of it for supper, with hot crunchy rolls and a hearty dessert. General Eisenhower, I hear, had a rule and a measure for every step of his soup, but mine grows as it goes.

There was the time when I was left to look after six children so that two sets of parents could go off to see a World Series game. A typewriter instead of a stove had been my familiar for so long just then that the problem of stoking those six stomachs for a whole week end appalled me a little—until I thought of vegetable soup. It could simmer while I typed and it would be good warmed over. Better. It was. My sister estimated afterward that there must have been six quarts to begin with. The children didn't complain more than usual—one of them was reputed to be no lover of soup, but she ate with the rest—and I had a good grist to show from the machine when the papas and the mamas returned.

There was that other time when I was leaving a garden, and home, for a long, long stay. I was never to see it again; nor to taste any more fruits at all of my father's raising. Though I did not fully sense the reason, there was a quality about the soup I made that autumn which I have never forgot—the garden had been particularly rewarding that year and father's pleasure in going with me to bring in the peppers and the cabbage and the other things he had grown was a deep, quiet feeling, expressed volubly only by his interest in the soup kettle.

It's the condiments one cannot buy, after all, that count the most and in an autumn soup there is the essence of all a season's work—the planting and the growth and the harvest.

CHAPTER 4

Onions for Their Own Sake

The various properties in onions make them a splendid substitute for meat when the price of steak and roast soars. Make the erstwhile garnish the star course and be thankful for vitamins in the earth and on your table.

A well-balanced menu for luncheon or dinner or a porch supper in summer can be arranged with any one of the onion dishes given in this chapter as the central feature, and a dessert adapted to the calories in the rest of the meal and in the main dish. Thus:

EGG CANAPÉ

BERMUDAS STUFFED WITH CHESTNUTS

(see page 41)

CORN MUFFINS

LETTUCE SALAD

GRAPE FRUIT Topped with Brown Sugar
and Brazil Nuts, Broiled

BEVERAGE

CREAMED ONIONS
#1

1 pound (about 12) small white onions
   or 6 medium size flat Spanish onions
2½ tsp. butter
½ tsp. salt
2 level tbsp. flour
⅛ tsp. black pepper
1 cup milk
¼ cup water

Peel onions under running water. Cut in about five slices each. Melt butter in an iron skillet, sprinkle salt on the onions, and cook over medium heat until they are golden brown, stirring occasionally. Add water, cover, and cook until onions are soft, about 15 minutes, stirring twice, with a wooden spoon.

Dust the flour lightly over the cooked onions, a little at a time to prevent lumping, stir again, and add milk which has been warmed. Cook until thick and well blended.

Onion moisture is variable with size and kind used. It will not spoil this dish if a little more milk is required to result in a smooth performance.

For a guest meal this recipe can be prepared the day before and reheated without spoiling the flavor.

A creamed vegetable like this is especially well suited to serve with meat dishes that have no gravy.

CREAMED ONIONS
#2

As one of the vegetables for Thanksgiving Dinner   For some this dish has only one interpretation—the traditional boiled onion in white sauce, to go with the turkey at the end of November. But it will be better tradition if you choose the sweet, purple-skinned onions that come from Italy and use some of the boiling liquid to make the cream sauce.

Allow three onions per person at most and at least ¼ cup of white sauce for each three onions. Boil them in salted water until tender. Test with a silver fork. If an onion is served only half cooked it is not wholly digestible. Don't make the guests' stomachs do part of the stove's work.

Drain the cooked onions thoroughly, else the extra liquid will thin the sauce too much.

Now prepare the white sauce. (See basic recipe on page 84). Brown the butter and flour slightly so that the finished dish will have a rich creamy look rather than the white gluey appearance that one associates with wallpaperer's paste.

When the sauce is ready and well seasoned with salt and pepper and a faint dash of nutmeg, heat the cooked onions in it until the sauce has been thoroughly laced with the onion flavor. Serve in a long soup tureen or covered vegetable dish—the best Haviland is none too good. Fleck the surface with a little fine black pepper.

ONIONS IN SOUR CREAM *

Count three onions per person at least, either the small sweet white ones (about twelve in a pound) or the yellow, mild Spanish. One cup of light sour cream will do for a pound.

Peel the onions, score tips, and cook in salted water until tender. Drain, return to the pan, and pour on the cream. Simmer over low heat until the cream is heated through and has absorbed the onion flavor fully.

Dust the top, when serving, with nutmeg or a very little mace. This is splendid with roast chicken.

* All references to sour cream mean dairy-soured and bought in a carton, light or heavy grade

GLACÉ ONIONS

    12 white onions, boiled until almost tender
     1 cup beef bouillon or consommé
     2 tbsp. butter (measured before melting)
     2 tbsp. finely sifted brown sugar

Brown onions in butter; pour on stock liquid and sprinkle with sugar. Cover and simmer down, basting occasionally, until the glaze adheres. Serve with roast pork.

PHILADELPHIA GLAZED ONIONS

Boil required number of onions, drain, and gently press dry between two layers of cheesecloth. Combine in a skillet 3 tbsp. butter and 2 tbsp. granulated sugar and, when melted, lay the onions in, turning frequently until completely glazed. This should be done over low heat so they will not brown too quickly.

BAKED GLAZED ONIONS

1 pound white onions
2 tbsp. butter
½ cup consommé
2 tbsp. water
1 tbsp. sugar
1 tbsp. flour
salt and pepper, q.s.

Prepare onions as for boiling. Melt butter in a heavy iron skillet and add consommé mixed with sugar and seasonings and simmer the onions gently until tender. Drain and transfer to a casserole. Combine flour and the two tablespoons of water, and blend with liquid in the pan until smooth. Pour over onions and bake 20 minutes.

CANDIED ONIONS

1 lb. small white onions
1 tbsp. sugar
½ tbsp. cornstarch
2 tbsp. cold water
½ cup grapefruit juice
1 tbsp. butter

Melt the butter in a heavy skillet, tilting it to be sure that entire surface and sides are coated. Sprinkle the peeled onions with the sugar, and add the fruit juice. Cover tightly and simmer 20 minutes or until onions are tender. Remove onions with a perforated spoon to a vegetable dish. Combine cornstarch and water and blend with the liquid remaining in the pan. Pour over onions and serve.

NOTE: If too much liquid has cooked away, add more fruit juice.

ONION PURÉE

This is a good base for soups, onion gravy to accompany a meat dish, casserole mixtures, soufflés, and onion custard.

> 2 cups sliced onions
> 2 cups boiling water
> 3 tbsp. butter
> 3 tbsp. flour

Cook the onions in the boiling water until they are tender. Sieve the whole and measure the resulting purée. Add enough consommé to make 1½ cups entire.

Make a *roux* of the butter and flour and blend with the onion mixture. Season to taste.

or

Start with the raw onions, sauté in butter, dust with flour and reduce with milk before forcing through the sieve.

NOTE: The consommé base is better for soups and gravy. Use the milk base for custards.

ONION CUSTARD

> 1 cup onion purée
> 2 eggs
> 1 tbsp. melted butter
> 2 rounded tbsp. flour
> 1 cup milk
> ⅛ tsp. black pepper
> ¼ tsp. salt
> ¼ tsp. nutmeg

Blend butter and flour and make a sauce with the milk. Add seasonings. Set aside to cool.

Combine beaten egg yolks with onion purée and add to the sauce. Fold in the stiffly beaten egg whites and pour all into a greased glass casserole or pottery baking dish. The custard should be firm in about 25 minutes in a moderate oven.

ONION SOUFFLÉ
#1

2 tbsp. flour
2 tbsp. butter
⅔ cup thin cream

Make a white sauce with these ingredients, which reduce the usual amount of liquid for white sauces. In this dish the beaten eggs provide the difference in liquid.

1 cup onion purée
3 egg yolks
3 egg whites
  seasonings as preferred

Heat white sauce and onion purée together, season if necessary and remove from fire. Have the egg yolks beaten and ready to stir in. When well blended, let this cool.

Then fold in the whites of the eggs beaten stiff.

Bake in a buttered soufflé dish for about a half hour at 350°. It should look dry and firm when done. Serve at once.

ONION SOUFFLÉ
#2

2 cups finely chopped yellow onions
5 tbsp. butter
1 cup chicken stock
4 eggs
  salt and pepper, q.s.

Melt butter in a saucepan, add onions and stir together over moderate heat until the onion is transparent. Add the flour and blend well. Pour in the stock and cook until the sauce is smooth, stirring to prevent sticking to the pan. Check seasoning.

Beat the eggs separately, adding the yolks to the sauce first. Then the egg whites, folded lightly into the whole.

Pour into an ungreased casserole, set in a pan of water and bake in a 350° oven until a silver knife inserted in the center comes out clean. This will take between an half and three-quarters of an hour.

GRILLED ONIONS

   3 large Bermuda onions
   ½ cup boiling water
   ½ cup butter, melted
     salt and pepper

Wash and peel onions; cut in slices ¼ inch thick. Arrange slices edge to edge in a shallow baking pan. Add water and cook in moderate oven for 15 minutes.

Drain carefully, brush with melted butter and broil under moderate heat, 5 minutes on each side. A pancake turner is useful for handling, so that the slices will not separate into rings. Serve in the baking dish, if it can go to the table, otherwise remove to a hot platter.

BROILED ONIONS ON TOAST

   3 large Bermuda onions
   1 cup grated Parmesan cheese
   ½ cup cooking oil

Slice onions thin enough that they will cook through without parboiling. Arrange on a long shallow glass baking dish. Brush with the oil and broil to a delicate brown on both sides, using a broad, short-bladed spatula to turn them and keep the slices intact. Toast rounds of bread cut a little larger than the onion slices. Butter one side, cover with a slice of onion, dust with the cheese, and paprika. Run under the broiler again before serving.

PAN BROILED

The flavor of these various grilled and panned onions more than makes up for the space taken in the oven. In this variant upon the two preceding recipes, the slices are cut ½ inch thick, spread with butter and seasonings, blended smoothly together. Add water, enough to cover the pan one-quarter inch, and bake, covered, until tender.

Serve with cold roast beef.

STUFFED ONIONS

Pour boiling water over the onions you wish to bake, four for four people, if large and not the main dish. Measure 1 tbsp. salt to each quart of water. Let the onions stand in this ten minutes.

Remove from the water and, when cool enough to handle, cut a slice from the top and remove center, leaving a thick-walled shell.

Fill with the mixture of your choice, packing down well and topping with buttered crumbs, crushed potato chips, or corn flakes.

Bake in a buttered casserole, covered, with a little water. Baste occasionally.

or

Peel the onions, make a slash criss-cross in the top, which will help keep the center in, and parboil 20 minutes in salted water. Drain and the center will be easily removable with a fork. Reserve centers to chop for soup.

FILLINGS AND TOPPINGS FOR ONION CASES

1. Substantial stuffings are recommended if the baked onions are to be a main dish.

2. Any finely chopped meat makes a hearty stuffing, such as sausage, corned beef hash, or ham with minced green pepper.

3. Rice combined with seasonings may be added to the chopped centers of the onions. Follow these proportions:

> ½ cup cooked rice
> ½ cup chopped nuts
> 1 tsp. Worcestershire Sauce
> ¼ tsp. chili powder
> salt to taste

4. Bread crumbs as a stuffing alone are impractical because the shells shrink a little in the baking and the center will be forced upward, spoiling the attractiveness of the dish. But crumbs may be used as a binding with other ingredients. A vegetable mixture contains bread crumbs in the following proportion:

> ⅓ cup minced celery
> 2 tbsp. melted butter
> 2 tbsp. chopped parsley
> 1½ cups breadcrumbs
> ½ cup chopped nuts
> season to taste

5. Chestnut Stuffing: Cut a ½-inch slit on the flat side of each nut. Use ½ tsp. fat to each cupful of nuts in a heavy frying pan. Shake the nuts in this over medium heat for five minutes. Or place for five minutes under the flame of the broiler. Remove shells and skins, which should come away together, with a sharp knife. Cover the shelled nuts with boiling water and cook for 15 minutes in a covered kettle. Test tenderness with a fork.

For onion stuffing, put through a ricer or fine sieve. To each cup of crumbled chestnuts add 1 tbsp. butter. Season with salt and pepper and beat until light, moistening with a little hot milk or cream if the mixture seems dry. Fill the onion cases and brush top with a little milk.

6. Buttered Bread Crumbs: Sauté 1 cup bread crumbs in ⅓ cup butter. This binds the crumbs together and is more satisfactory

than sprinkling them dry on top of a baked dish and dotting with butter.

Cheese grated, with a little crumbled bacon added, and combined with the crumbs is a good variant. Reduce amount of butter with the crumbs if using bacon.

Crush cheesed cocktail crackers and moisten with a little milk. Run under broiler if casserole is already cooked, to brown the top.

BAKED ONIONS

Onions can be baked in their skins. Wipe them, without peeling and bake as you would potatoes. It takes about an hour and an half in a moderate oven.

When cool enough to handle, cut a slice from the root end, and shell out the moist inner layers and heart of the onion. These may be dressed in any way one likes, with a seasoned butter dressing, or with crumbled cheese.

FRENCH FRIED ONIONS

A red-skinned Spanish onion is best for deep fat frying. If yellow ones must be used, soak in milk for a half hour. Drain before dusting with flour.

Do not fill frying kettle more than half full with oil or melted fat. Peanut oil is recommended highly for this purpose. When onions are added, any oil will boil up a little higher in the kettle because of their moisture content.

Serve as soon as possible after cooking. Don't cover if there is any delay, or they will get limp.

Fried in Batter: This can be made with 1 egg yolk, ½ cup milk, ½ cup flour, and salt. Dip the onions, in rings or in quarter chunks, in the batter and then in deep fat at 395° and cook about five minutes.

Fry only a few onion rings at a time and drain on paper.

PAN FRIED ONIONS IN SLICES

    6 large Bermuda onions
    ¼ cup water
    6 tbsp. butter
      salt and pepper, q.s.

Slice the onions, about ¾ inches thick, and peel. This saves time. Cook in a chicken fryer with the water until they are tender, seasoning at once.

Drain off any excess water and add the butter. Brown the onions, being careful not to break the slices. Turn them over after five minutes, when they should be deep golden, with a wide short spatula and a pie server, to keep the slices whole. Scatter the pepper on the second side.

Use this form of fried onion with steak or liver or any meat course without gravy.

PAN FRIED ONIONS

Follow the same procedure as in first recipe, but slice the onions and cook in butter, over low heat, stirring until well browned. Serve with steak or liver.

FRENCH FRIED SCALLIONS

Prepare scallions as for serving raw. Cut into little finger lengths, roll in egg and crumbs and fry in deep fat.

SCALLOPED ONIONS WITH CHEESE

    1½ lbs. white onions
     4 tbsp. butter
     4 tbsp. flour
     2 cups milk
     ¼ tsp. paprika

1 tsp. salt
¼ tsp. celery salt
½ tsp. mustard
½ cup cheese, cut fine

Make a sauce in top of a double boiler, of the butter, flour and milk. When well blended add seasonings and cheese and cook until the latter has melted.

When the onions have been parboiled, with crosscuts in the top to keep them whole, and a dash of lemon in the water to keep them white, drain and place in large buttered casserole. Pour the sauce over them, cover with buttered crumbs, and bake about an half hour, or until onions test tender to silver fork.

This is a better dish if the cheese is sharp.

VARIANTS

Onions have been successfully scalloped with green peppers and with eggplant. (See pages 53, 54.)

ONIONS AU GRATIN

2 Bermuda onions
2 hard-cooked eggs
¼ tsp. salt
1 tbsp. minced parsley
1 cup Sauce Veloute (see page 85) or plain white sauce

Peel and slice the onions, and cook in salted water until almost tender.

Mash the yolks of the eggs, season, and combine with white sauce and the parsley.

Add the sliced onions, drained, to avoid thinning the sauce, and bake in individual ramekins, topping with cheesed bread-crumbs. Bake about 20 minutes and if the tops are not brown enough, run under the broiler flame before serving.

FRENCH CASSEROLE ONIONS

Select two Bermuda onions a little smaller in diameter than an individual, side-handled earthenware casserole.

Prepare as for plain boiled, cutting off root slice and tip, and cross-slashing to keep center in. Cook until almost done in boiling salted water. Drain and cool.

Hold with a piece of cheesecloth while cutting cross-wise in half with a sharp knife. Place each half in a greased casserole. Fill to brim with condensed mushroom soup thinned with a little milk, top with buttered crumbs and bake until the onions are tender to silver fork.

CHAPTER 5

With Other Vegetables

Onions belong with some things in the same way that there is a debit for every credit in double-entry bookkeeping, or a button for every buttonhole. The way a baby needs its mother. She brings out the best in the baby. One of the most satisfying properties of the onion, which chemists can't isolate, is its grace, like a mother, in bringing out the flavor of anything with which it is combined, while not too aggressively asserting its own. Its presence in proper ratio enhances the pleasant bite of other ingredients in a dish. If your onions with green beans, or in brussels sprouts, or smothering eggplant, shout aloud, then you haven't been subtle enough. Check the ratio and try again.

Onions share a flavor rôle with salt, performing the same office for mild vegetables that spices do in pickle. Most of us will admit that the human animal is inconsistent nine-tenths of the time, but do not realize that we are so at table, eating because we like the flavor or the odor of food, rather than because it is good for us. If onions in new guises can make us like the things that are good for us, why worry about the state of Public Health?

SCALLOP OF APPLES AND ONIONS

> 4 cooking apples, green variety preferably
> 4 yellow onions, medium size
> ½ cup flour
> 4 tbsp. finely sifted brown sugar
> ½ tsp. salt

47

¼ tsp. nutmeg
1 cup water

Mix water and flour with seasonings to make a thin sauce. Peel apples and onions. Slice them crosswise. Lay in buttered casserole in alternate layers dressed with liquid between. Top with buttered corn flakes. Bake until tender to silver fork.

Check liquid during baking. If the apples are on the dry side, it may be necessary to add a little water.

FRIED ONIONS WITH APPLES

4 onions, yellow preferred
3 large tart apples, greenings are best
2 tbsp. fat (butter or bacon)
½ tsp. salt
½ cup water
2 tbsp. sugar

Peel and slice the onions. Wash apples; core and slice but do not peel.

Melt the fat in a frying pan and cook the onions alone until nearly tender. Add apples to onions and pour over the salted water. Cover and cook until the apples are soft.

Remove cover and sprinkle with sugar. Cook until the water is all absorbed. The onions and apples should be a light brown.

ARTICHOKES AND ONION

Flavor globe artichokes with a thick slice of onion in the boiling water.

ONIONS AND BAKED BEANS

Bury one good-sized Spanish onion, peeled but whole, in the beans you bake for the week end. Pour on a tablespoon or two of grape juice.

This, with the onion, will beat down the path to your door that Emerson predicted. She who makes better baked beans . . . though she live in the woods . . . Well, the beans will be eaten.

WITH GREEN BEANS AND BACON

1 lb. fresh green beans
2 strips bacon
2 small white onions

Cook the beans in boiling salted water until tender, in the usual way.

Fry the bacon until it will crumble easily. Remove from fat and drain.

Peel and dice the onion and sauté in the bacon fat, being careful not to burn any of the small pieces.

Toss the drained beans in the onioned fat, heat through again, and serve, garnished with the crisp bacon.

ONIONS WITH GREEN BEANS AU GRATIN

1 lb. green string beans
3 Spanish onions
1 egg yolk
1 cup white sauce
½ cup bread crumbs and dry grated cheese
1 bay leaf
¼ cup coarsely chopped parsley
    salt, pepper and paprika to make ¼ tsp.

String the beans and snap into inch lengths. Peel and quarter the onions. Cook together, with bay leaf and parsley in boiling salted water until tender. Drain, keeping the liquid for future soup.

Beat the egg yolk and blend with the white sauce. Arrange layers of beans and the onion quarters (which have probably separated in the cooking) in a glass baking dish and pour over sufficient sauce to cover. Top with the cheesed crumbs and bake for about 20 minutes or until brown.

BAKED LIMA BEANS WITH SPANISH ONION

1 pint dried lima beans
2 quarts water
¼ pound salt pork, diced
1 tbsp. brown sugar, sifted fine

2 tbsp. butter
2 Spanish onions, medium size
salt, pepper and paprika

Soak beans over night in cold water. Drain, cover with two quarts fresh water, add the diced pork and cook slowly, uncovered, until the beans are tender. The beans should be mealy and the liquid cooked down to a thick sauce.
Check seasonings.
Turn into shallow baking dish and cover entire top with the onion, sliced ¼″ thick. Add a little water.
Bake in moderate oven till juice has cooked down again and onion is tender and brown. Sprinkle with paprika before serving.

ONIONS AND BEETS OVEN BOILED

Pare and dice enough beets to make 2 cups—about three medium-sized beets. Halve onions crosswise and quarter, in about the same proportion, to make two cups. Toss together in a large casserole, season with 1½ tsp. salt and 2 tbsp. butter melted in 4 tbsp. boiling water.
Cover the casserole and cook in moderate oven, until beets test tender to silver fork. It will take about an hour.

ONIONS BAKED WITH BRUSSELS SPROUTS

1 cup cooked sprouts
1 cup small white onions, cooked whole
½ can condensed pea soup
¼ cup thin cream (4 tbsp.)
4 tbsp. cooking water from the sprouts
¼ tsp. curry powder
½ tsp. condiment sauce (optional)
add salt if necessary

Arrange the sprouts and onions in a casserole. Blend liquids and seasonings. Pour over the sprouts and onions and garnish with four strips of cooked bacon. Bake in moderate oven until the mixture bubbles.

BRUSSELS SPROUTS AND ONIONS IN CREAM

Boil sprouts and onions. Use part of cooking water for liquid in white sauce made with light cream. Serve with cold meat.

ONIONS IN BAKED CORN PUDDING

    1 cup canned corn, cream style
    1 cup milk
    2 tbsp. flour
    1 tbsp. butter, melted
    2 eggs
    1 Spanish onion, minced
    1 tsp. salt
    1 tsp. black pepper
    ½ tsp. paprika

Beat the yolks of the eggs in a mixing bowl; season the corn with ½ tsp. salt, the pepper and paprika, and the onion; blend with the egg yolks.

Pour on the sauce which has previously been made and set to cool (milk, flour, butter and ½ tsp. salt).

Beat the egg whites stiff and fold into the mixture.

Bake in a greased glass casserole in a moderate oven until the pudding is set. The top should be smooth and brown as in a soufflé.

ONION IN CORN FRITTERS

    1 cup canned corn
    2 tbsp. butter
    2 tbsp. flour
    1 tsp. salt
    ¼ tsp. paprika
    ½ cup milk
    1 egg
    1 tsp. baking powder
    2 tbsp. minced Spanish onion

Beat the egg yolk until thick in a mixing bowl; add corn and melted butter. Blend dry ingredients with flour and stir in. Thin with the milk to make a batter, and drop by spoonfuls into hot cooking fat.

These are sometimes called corn oysters. Brown on both sides, and drain on paper. Keep hot until ready to serve. Do not cover or they will lose their crispness.

BRAISED CELERY WITH ONIONS

1 large bunch Pascal celery
1½ cups consommé or beef bouillon
1 yellow onion
2 tbsp. butter

Cut off the root end of the celery; remove leafy tops evenly; peel root and reserve for salad. Cook tops and a few leaves for soup stock.

Separate bunch, wash and scrape until clean.

Chop onion, but do not mince, and sauté in butter in a heavy skillet until transparent. Lay celery stalks on top and pour in the consommé. Cover and cook slowly over a low flame until the celery is soft and has absorbed all the liquid. Serve with steak.

CUCUMBERS IN SOUR CREAM WITH ONIONS

1 firm medium sized cucumber
2 small sweet white onions
¼ cup sour cream
¼ cup prepared hollandaise sauce
½ cup herb vinegar or lemon juice
salt and pepper
parsley, fresh dill, or caraway seed

Peel the cucumber and onions and slice thin. Marinate for two hours in the vinegar or seasoned lemon juice. Pour off the liquid that has not soaked in.

Combine hollandaise and sour cream and toss the cucumber and onions in it until well coated.

Garnish and serve as accompaniment to cold meat, as a hearty hors d'oeuvre or as filling for a rye sandwich.

ONIONS WITH EGGPLANT

1 medium-sized eggplant
½ lb. small white onions
3 ripe tomatoes
1 small carton light sour cream
   salt, black pepper, curry powder
   cooking oil or butter

Peel eggplant and sauté in sticks or cubes. Remove from skillet and place in bottom of a large greased baking dish.

Peel and slice onions and sauté until partly cooked, taking care to keep the slices whole. Cover the eggplant with onions.

Slice the tomatoes and fry, after rolling in seasoned flour. Add these to the casserole.

Heat sour cream and cover the vegetables. Bake in a moderate oven until cream is absorbed and a silver fork tests tender.

ONION AND OKRA HASH

With kitchen scissors, clip three pieces of bacon in inch pieces, and brown in an iron skillet. Dice two medium-sized yellow or white onions and cook with bacon until tender. Add a pound of fresh okra pods which have been washed and tipped and cut into ½ inch lengths. Season with salt and pepper.

Stir occasionally and, when the okra begins to change color and can be easily cut through, add 1¾ cups canned tomatoes mixed with 1 tbsp. sugar and cook down, simmering until thick.

Serve with Vienna bread, or hard rolls, or a large bowl of plain boiled rice.

FRESH GREEN PEAS
(Following French Method)

2 lbs. fresh green peas
1 large crisp leaf iceberg lettuce
¼ tsp. table salt
½ tsp. evaporated onion salt, or
1 tsp. onion flakes, or
1 small onion, minced

Shell peas, break up lettuce and cook both with seasonings in a heavy steel kettle, just covered with boiling water, until peas are tender. About 15 minutes.

Drain, saving water for soup stock. Remove lettuce.

Sprinkle peas with a pinch of black pepper, add 1 tbsp. butter, cover again and let stand long enough for butter to melt, before serving.

SCALLIONS WITH GREEN PEAS

2 lbs. fresh green peas
2 tbsp. butter
1 cup finely shredded lettuce (½ a small head)
3 scallions, cleaned and chopped
1 tsp. sugar
½ tsp. salt
¼ tsp. black pepper
⅛ tsp. nutmeg
¼ cup boiling water.

Shell peas. Sauté lettuce and scallions in the butter, until clear. Combine seasonings, blend with sauté, and add peas and water.

Cook until peas are tender (12 to 20 minutes) and liquid is absorbed.

SCALLOPED ONIONS WITH GREEN PEPPERS

¾ lb. white onions
4 sweet green peppers
3 tbsp. butter
2 cups white sauce *
¼ lb. cheddar cheese

Peel onions and parboil whole, following usual boiling directions.

Remove seeds and membrane from peppers and cut crosswise in rings. Halve the rings and sauté in butter.

Arrange onions and peppers in layers in a large casserole and pour over the white sauce.

Top with breadcrumbs and thin slices of the cheese. Bake until heated through and cheese melts.

* See Sauce Veloute page 85.

ONIONS IN POTATO BATTER

This is really a fritter. Run potatoes through an electric blender for best results.

> 1 cup potato, finely shredded
> 1 egg
> 4 tbsp. flour
> ½ tsp. salt
> 1 cup white onions, sliced
> ¾ cup cooking oil or melted fat

Beat egg in a mixing bowl; blend flour and salt. Add potato to the egg and then the dry ingredients. This mixture should be of batter consistency.

Heat the cooking oil or fat in a skillet, dip onions in the batter and fry on both sides until browned. Drain and sprinkle with a little salt.

KATIE'S CASSEROLE

Count one small potato and one medium sized onion per person. Or, four each for four people, as here.

Butter a large casserole, *including lid*. Pare and slice thin both onions and potatoes. Arrange in layers, seasoning with salt, pepper and butter between each two layers, until casserole is filled. Pour on milk until ⅔ of the dish is filled.

Cover and cook in slow oven (300°) about two hours.

This recipe was given me a long time ago by a friend who has unique food sense. One could almost believe that the rare direction to butter the lid is the secret of this dish. Rather, it's in the slow cooking and, when Katie does it, it's flavored with the joy she puts into it. Yours can be *almost* as good as hers, without that condiment.

ORDINARY POTATO SCALLOP

Prepare as usual but use canned cream of onion soup for the liquid, diluted slightly with milk.

SKILLET SCALLOP

This is a cross between potatoes creamed raw in milk, and a real scallop.

        4 potatoes
        2 between-size onions
        2 tbsp. butter
        2 cups milk
          seasonings

Peel onions and potatoes and slice thin. Melt part of the butter in the skillet, lay in alternating layers of the vegetables, and season and dot with the rest of the butter on the way.

Pour in the milk, heat to boiling point, reduce fire, and cook until potatoes are soft.

STUFFED POTATOES WITH VARIATIONS

Bake potatoes, remove centers, whip as for mashed, and return to shell.

1. Add chopped chives to the whipping operation.
2. Garnish with french fried onion rings.
3. Rub the bowl with garlic before you begin to whip the centers.
4. Make a little hollow in the mound of beaten potato and fill with creamed onion.
5. Blend a little paprika and onion salt and dust over the tops of the filled shells.
6. There is also onion salt for seasoning within.

OHIO PANCAKES

        2 large raw potatoes
        1 mild onion
        ½ tsp. salt
        1 tbsp. flour
        1 egg
          pinch black pepper

Grate the potatoes, or put them in an electric blender; chop the onion or blend it; make a batter of the other ingredients and combine. Fry in hot cooking oil, or vegetable shortening.

BETTY'S POTATO PUFFS

1 cup soft, fluffy mashed potatoes
½ cup sifted flour
1 tsp. baking powder
1 egg, beaten slightly
¼ tsp. salt
1 tbsp. minced seasonal onion
1 tsp. minced parsley
frying fat

Sift salt, flour and baking powder together. Combine potatoes, egg, onion, and parsley. Blend together, and drop by spoonfuls into an iron skillet, in which about ¼ inch fat is heated. Brown on one side and turn as for potato cakes. This is a good alternative to deep fat frying.

DUTCH SAUERKRAUT

4 cups kraut
1 large apple
1 Bermuda onion
1 medium sized potato
2 tbsp. bacon fat
½ cup hot water

Combine sauerkraut with apple and onion, which have been peeled and quartered. Add water to cover and simmer 1½ hours. Drain.

Grate potato and mix with sauerkraut, together with bacon fat and hot water, and simmer again 30 minutes. Stir frequently.

Serve with sausages.

STUFFED ACORN SQUASH

2 acorn squash
6 tbsp. minced Spanish onion
4 tbsp. butter
1½ tsp. salt
¼ tsp. pepper
2 tbsp. cream

Wash squash and cut in two lengthwise. Remove seed and membrane center. Cook in boiling salted water until tender.

Meantime, prepare the stuffing: sauté onion in butter, but do not brown.

When squash is done, remove from water and drain. Scoop out soft centers. Add minced onion, cooked, with seasonings and cream, and whip. Pile in the shells, and dust with paprika before running under the broiler to brown.

YELLOW SQUASH AU GRATIN

2 squashes
1 cup rich white sauce
1 yellow onion
2 egg yolks
2 tbsp. grated cheese
½ cup bread crumbs
⅛ tsp. nutmeg
1 tbsp. chopped parsley

Wash squash and cube without peeling. Quarter the onion. Cook in boiling salted water with the parsley until tender.

Beat egg yolks and blend with the white sauce.

Drain squash and onion. Fold into the sauce mixture and pour all into a glass casserole.

Combine crumbs and cheese and cover the top, baking until brown, about a half hour.

WHOLE ONIONS IN TOMATO SHELLS

Select onions slightly smaller than the tomatoes to be stuffed. Prepare tomato shells as for any mixture, and drain. Parboil the onions, set inside the salted tomatoes, dot each with butter, and salt and pepper, and set in a baking dish with a small amount of water. Bake until onions are tender.

FRIED TOMATOES WITH ONION GRAVY

This is an end-of-the-summer dish when the tomatoes can be carried from the garden to the kitchen, with no halts on the way.

4 firm ripe tomatoes
4 tbsp. butter or bacon fat
2 tbsp. minced seasonal onion
1 cup coffee cream
    salt, pepper, paprika, q.s.

Slice the tomatoes rather thick but do not peel. Coat with seasoned flour, and brown in the fat on both sides, removing to a hot platter until all are cooked. It may be necessary to add a little fat from time to time, and there should be enough left in the pan in which to cook the minced onion. Stir well through the fat and the crusty bits remaining, and return all the tomatoes to the pan, pouring in the cream to just cover. Simmer until the cream and flour jackets on the tomatoes are blended into a thick sauce. Serve hot.

STEWED TOMATOES WITH ONIONS

This dish will bear the cream treatment remarkably well. Chop three white onions in the next stewed tomatoes you cook up for an emergency vegetable—stewed tomatoes are only that, unless they are toned a little. Cook the onion separately until tender, combine with the stew and add 4 tbsp. cream. Check seasonings and serve when thick.

ONION BUTTER

A good seasoning combination for fresh cooked vegetables to be dressed with butter is as follows:
For each cupful of the plain boiled vegetable combine
    1 tsp. butter or cream
    ⅛ tsp. salt
    ¼ tsp. onion salt
    ⅛ tsp. black pepper
        paprika, optional
                or
Substitute minced fresh onion for the onion salt, a scant teaspoon per cup of vegetable and sauté in the butter before adding dry seasoning.

CHAPTER 6

With Bread and Pastry

There is an old story, so old it has a beard, which makes it new, about two travelers in the Southern hills who stopped at a remote cabin and asked for corn bread. The delighted hostess said, "Co'n braid, co'n braid, 's all we ain't got anything else but. Light, stranger, light and set."

It is unbelievable that she didn't have onions, or that they wouldn't have tasted like some of these, with the corn bread baked on a hoe on her hearth, no doubt, and no sugar in it.

SKILLET CORN BREAD

1½ cups sifted flour
¾ cup corn meal
3½ tsp. baking powder
3 tbsp. sugar
1 tsp. salt
6 tbsp. butter, melted
1 egg, well beaten
1 cup milk
1 medium sized onion, minced

Sift dry ingredients together. Cook minced onion in a little of the butter. Remove and add to beaten egg, milk, and the rest of the butter, melted. Blend with flour mixture, pour all into the greased skillet and bake in a hot oven, 400°, from 25 to 30 minutes.

ONION SHORTCAKES

Shortcake is a harp with many strings. The cake part can be biscuit dough in its many varieties or corn bread, Northern journey cake and Southern, without sugar. And whether biscuit or corn bread it can be baked in individual form or in one large sheet to be split in layers, covered with the chosen top and cut at the table in serving portions.

This is a substantial dish and can be used as the center of a party breakfast, a home luncheon or a Sunday night supper in winter.

For baking powder biscuit dough, use the recipe on page 154, omitting chives.

Here is a basic corn bread recipe.

JOURNEY CAKE

- 1 cup yellow corn meal
- 1 cup all purpose white flour (sifted before measuring)
- 1 tsp. salt
- 1 tbsp. sugar
- 2 rounded tsp. baking powder
- 2 eggs
- 3 tbsp. butter
- 1 cup milk

Sift all dry ingredients together. Melt butter and add to beaten eggs, then the milk and pour all into the seasoned flours, blending quickly. Batter should be thin. Bake in a greased layer cake pan in a hot oven, about a half hour.

VARIANTS

1. Make a sheet of journey cake, cut in squares, split each with a cake divider and spread with the filling of the day.

2. Buy corn muffins at the grocery store, six in a box and good, whether you use them as Nature meant or for a shortcake short-cut. They're wonderful.

3. Double the quantity of the one-cup-of-flour biscuit recipe on page 154 and that will be enough for six individual shortcakes. Cut twelve rings with a large-size biscuit cutter, brush half of them with a little melted butter, top each with one of the remaining rounds, and bake on a cookie sheet in a quick oven— about 12 minutes. They will split easily with a fork at the division. Serve these suggested bases with any of the following:

a. The creamed onions, recipe No. 1 in Chapter 4 (page 34), with a little mustard added.

b. Flavor one can condensed mushroom soup with finely chopped onion, cooked in butter until clear. Dilute less than for soup and heat. Spread on individual shortcakes and top each with a bacon curl and a parsley leaf.

c. Fry tomatoes which have been dipped in seasoned flour in onion-or-garlic-flavored fat. When crisp and brown, use one slice for the middle of each shortcake, either biscuit or corn bread, and cover with a sauce made from the gravy fat, remaining in the pan, with a little flour and cream added.

d. Use biscuit dough flavored with chives and cover with a cream, dried beef gravy to which has been added a few fresh mushrooms chopped and cooked with a little salt and nutmeg.

HUSH PUPPIES

$1\frac{1}{2}$ cups corn meal
$1\frac{1}{2}$ cups flour
3 eggs
3 tbsp. baking powder
3 tbsp. sugar
1 tsp. salt
$\frac{1}{4}$ tsp. pepper
3 tbsp. minced onion
water to make a stiff dough

Drop by ½ tsp. in hot deep fat. Heat the spoon in the fat before dipping up the next one, and the puppy will slide off better and be less inclined to break.

ONIONS IN CORN DODGERS

1 cup cornmeal
3 tbsp. butter
2 sweet white onions, small
¼ cup milk
2 cups water
1 tsp. salt
pinch black pepper

Mince the onions coarsely and sauté until clear in 1 tbsp. butter, seasoning a little.

Melt the remaining butter in a heavy saucepan, and add water and the rest of the seasoning. When it boils, sift in the cornmeal, stirring at the same time and until well blended. Cook for about 20 minutes, stirring again from time to time to prevent lumps.

Then add the onions and the scalded milk and cook until thick enough to drop by spoonfuls on a buttered cookie sheet. This will take about five minutes.

Bake in a very hot oven. Should be done in 15 minutes.

SALMON CORN CAKES WITH ONION RINGS

1 cup corn meal
1 cup boiling water
1 tsp. salt
1 egg
1 cup flaked canned salmon
1 Bermuda onion

Slice the onion, remove outer shell and separate the rest in rings. Crisp them in a bowl of ice water. Drain and dry when ready to garnish the plate of salmond cakes.

Sift the corn meal into the boiling water, to which salt has been added. Cook until it begins to thicken. Set aside to cool.

Mix together the well-beaten egg and the salmon and combine with the corn meal dough to make patties. Fry on both sides in hot fat.

Serve with chili sauce.

SPOON BREAD WITH ONIONS

    2 cups white corn meal
    2 cups boiling water
    1 tsp. salt
    3 tbsp. butter, melted
 1½ cups sweet milk
    3 eggs
    4 tbsp. minced yellow onion

Sift corn meal twice and sift into boiling salted water for a third time, stirring until smooth.

Add onion, butter, and heated milk. Beat eggs separately. Add yolks first, then fold in the whites and pour mixture into a buttered glass baking dish. In a moderate oven, 350°, it will take about 45 minutes. Serve at table by spoonfuls from the baking dish.

ONION UPSIDE DOWN CAKE

    6 medium size Spanish onions
    3 tbsp. butter
    2 cups flour, measured after sifting
    4 tsp. baking powder
    1 tsp. salt
    1 tsp. sugar
    1 egg, beaten
 1¼ cups milk

Slice onions and sauté in butter until yellow and soft. Let cool a little. Keep in slices if possible.

Make a batter of other ingredients, by sifting all the dry things together, and adding milk. The batter should be a little thinner than biscuit dough. Spread onions in a greased baking dish, slice touching slice. Pour dough on top. Bake 25 to 35 minutes in a moderate oven.

Serve with roast beef.

ONION BISCUITS

> 2 cups sliced onions (see measurements, end paper)
> 2 tbsp. butter
> 1 egg
> ½ cup light sour cream
> ½ tsp. salt
> Double recipe for biscuit dough on page 154, without chives

Make dough first and pat into a square glass baking dish or cake pan, thinner in the middle. Brush with a little melted butter or beaten egg white to prevent sogginess when custard is poured in.

Cook onions in the butter until they begin to brown, seasoning slightly with salt and a little pepper if desired.

Blend egg and cream.

Spread the cooked onions on the dough and pour the liquid on top, to bake in a very hot oven until custard is set and browning. About 20 minutes.

Cut in squares and serve with any hot meat.

BREAD AND ONION CUSTARD WITH CHEESE

> 1 cup sharp cheese cut in small slices
> 2 eggs
> 2 cups milk
> 1 Spanish onion
> 1 tbsp. butter
> ½ small loaf white bread

Peel and mince the onion and sauté in the butter until clear. Remove crusts from the bread and cut in one-inch cubes.

Butter a baking dish and place in it alternate layers of bread, cheese slices and onion, seasoning with salt and paprika.

Combine the beaten eggs with the milk, pour over the whole and bake about a half hour or until the custard is set.

POULTRY DRESSINGS

They call it *dressing* in the *Midwest*. In Vermont they *stuff* with *dressing*. In Philadelphia it's *filling,* though elsewhere in Pennsylvania cooks call the same thing a *stuffing,* as they do in Dixie. Some of us, I shouldn't wonder, are calling it that because they did so in Scotland in the 1700's. Like the rose, it's the same, whatever the generic term and it smells just as good, the ones with onions, the best of all.

Always sauté onions in butter before mixing with other ingredients for a dressing.

Two slices of bread make 1 cup of cubes.

WITH SAGE AND ONIONS

> 2 cups stale bread cubes
> 1 cup hot water or stock
> 1 egg
> ½ tsp. black pepper
> 2 tsp. chopped parsley
>   pinch dried sage
> 1 tsp. salt
> 4 tbsp. butter
> 4 white onions

Parboil the onions, or chop and sauté in some of the butter. Beat the egg, add bread cubes and stock in which all the seasonings have been mixed, and combine. Add the melted butter.

Two cups of creamy mashed potatoes can be substituted for the bread, checking seasoning.

This amount will do for a small chicken.

GIBLET DRESSING

Amounts given are for a ten-pound turkey.

  3 tbsp. minced onion
  ½ cup fat
  12 cups crumbled bread
  ¼ cup chopped parsley
  1 tbsp. poultry seasoning
  additional salt and pepper if needed
  turkey giblets chopped

Sauté giblets and onion in hot fat. Add to bread crumbs. Combine parsley and other seasonings and add to first mixture. Moisten with a little giblet stock, if necessary.

SOUTHERN STYLE

  4 cups corn bread crumbs
  1 cup pecans, chopped
  4 strips bacon
  1 cup chopped celery
  1 cup onions sliced thin
  2 eggs
  1½ tsp. salt
  ½ tsp. pepper
  1 tsp. sage
  ½ tsp. thyme
  2 tbsp. minced parsley

Combine corn bread, nuts, seasonings and parsley. Fry bacon slowly until crisp and crumble into first mixture. Sauté celery and onion in bacon drippings but do not brown. Add to mixing bowl and pour over all the eggs, beaten lightly.

This should be enough to stuff a four-pound chicken.

BRAZIL NUT

  3 cups stale bread cubes
  1 cup chopped Brazil nuts

½ cup finely chopped celery
2 tbsp. minced onion
3 tbsp. butter
1 tsp. salt
⅛ tsp. pepper
½ tsp. poultry seasoning or preferred combination

Melt butter in a kettle; add onion, celery, and some of the seasoning and cook over low heat until both are soft. Add bread cubes, nuts, remaining seasoning, and stir until thoroughly mixed.

For a moist stuffing, bind with a little water. Sufficient for a five-pound bird.

PASTRY

CRUST FOR 9-INCH PIE

1 cup sifted all purpose flour
½ tsp. salt
⅓ cup shortening
2-3 tbsp. ice water

Sift salt and flour together into a mixing bowl.

Measure shortening by filling a measuring cup 2/3 full with ice water. Add shortening until water reaches cup level and pour off.

Add half of the shortening to the flour and salt, blending with two knives or a pastry blender, until the mixture looks like meal. This is done for tenderness. Add remaining shortening, proceeding as before, until the particles are the size of large peas. You should have a flaky crust as a result.

Sprinkle the ice water lightly over the mixture. Blend it gently with a fork. Too much water makes pastry tough. Just enough should be used to enable you to gather the dough together with the fingers so its cleans the bowl.

Mound the dough on a floured board and roll out, keeping it in a circle as far as possible. To transfer to pie pan, fold sheet of pastry in half, lift it quickly and unfold it in the pan. Fit and trim.

If the dough is prepared a day before needed, and chilled in the refrigerator, the crust will be even more flaky and tender.

AUNT MARY'S ONION PIE

    9 medium sized Spanish onions
    2 tbsp. salt
    4 tbsp. butter
    ⅛ lb. butter
    3 eggs
    1 cup sweet cream
    3 strips lean bacon

Peel and slice onions, sprinkle with salt and let stand for a half hour. Make pastry for a 9-inch single crust pie.

Squeeze moisture from onions with your hands. Sauté the onions in butter until fairly brown, when all butter should be absorbed, and spread evenly on the crust.

Beat the eggs as for any custard, a little more than slightly. Blend eggs and cream and pour the mixture over the onions. Cut the bacon in narrow strips and arrange on top.

Bake 45 minutes in 400° oven or until the crust is golden brown and the custard has set firmly.

Serve hot.

BROILED ONION PIE

    6 medium size yellow or red onions
    2 tbsp. butter
    1¼ cups whole milk or
    1 cup half and half
    1 egg
    1 tbsp. flour
    ½ tsp. salt
    ½ tsp. pepper

Peel and slice the onions. Sauté in the butter until soft.

Make sauce of the flour, 4 tbsp. milk, and seasonings. Beat egg, combine with remaining milk, and add to the sauce. Stir into the onion mixture, cook until well blended, and pour all into a freshly baked pie shell. Run under broiler to set and brown on top.

TWO CRUST ONION PIE

Double crust for a 9-inch pie
3 large onions
8 tbsp. butter
4 tbsp. flour
1 cup coffee cream or whole milk
2 eggs
   seasoning, choice and q.s.

Peel and chop the onions. Sauté in the butter until tender. Sprinkle with the flour and seasonings and blend. Add the liquid and stir until thick. Remove from the fire and combine with the well-beaten eggs.

With half of the pastry dough rolled to fit, line a pan or glass pie dish. It is not necessary to grease the dish, but brush a little melted butter over the crust to prevent sogginess when the pie is baked.

Pour the cooked mixture into the pastry, cover with the top crust, and bake in a hot oven for about an half hour, or until a silver knife thrust through the steam vent in the top crust comes away clean, showing that the custard is set.

This pie should be served hot, as a main dish, or with a roast and a green salad. No dessert, I should say, though possibly coffee will be called for.

FILLED ONION TARTS

4 medium sized Spanish onions
2 tbsp. butter
¼ cup cold water
⅛ tsp. nutmeg
½ tsp. salt
½ tsp. minced parsley
   pastry for one pie crust

Peel onions and chop fine. Sauté in the butter until they commence to clear, stirring with a wooden spoon. Add seasonings and, when they are well blended, the water, and simmer until both water and butter are absorbed. The amount will cook down considerably. Cool.

Roll out the crust very thin and cut in rounds with a 1¾-inch cutter. On half of the rounds spread 1 tsp. of the onion mixture. Cover with the rest of the rounds, on the principle of a filled cooky and press down the edges firmly together.

Bake until crust is well done. You should have about 16 small tarts.

LITTLE ONION PIES
#1

The one-crust recipe for a 9-inch pie will make 6 small pies. Prepare the dough the day before and chill in the refrigerator, letting it come to room temperature again before attempting to roll it out.

Prepare the 6 patty pans or a tray of 6 gem pans with the individual crusts before making the filling.

    1 tbsp. butter
    3 tbsp. grated or finely minced onion
  1¾ cups sharp cheese, cut fine
    6 egg yolks
      salt, pepper and nutmeg to taste
    2 cups light coffee cream or whole milk

Cook the onion in the butter, stirring until light golden color. Cool and add the cheese. Set aside.

Beat eggs and cream and seasonings together until thoroughly blended.

Brush each shell with melted butter and place in it a spoonful of the onion and cheese mixture. Cover with the liquid, dot each pie with a small piece of butter to prevent the thick scum that arises on custards, and bake until it is firm and golden.

LITTLE ONION PIES
#2

For a buffet supper, prepare creamed onions, sauté, and serve in pastry shells. These go well with cold sliced ham, a fruit and avocado salad and a light dessert. Dust tops with paprika.

SHAKER PUDDING

This is a very old recipe given to me verbatim out of an ancient record, and included here principally for its amusement value. The comment with it ran that it was a "nice dish for visitors" when it came into my clutching hand. It is a pity that there were no directions with it for combining the ingredients. Even so it is a nice suggestion with which to end a chapter.

> ½ lb. butternuts
> ¼ lb. bread crumbs
> ¼ lb. butter
> ½ tsp. baking powder
> ½ tsp. salt

Very small onion cut *very* fine. Bake in small pie dishes.

CHAPTER 7

In Sauces
and Dressings

A true sauce is meant only to accompany a meat or a vegetable and never to disguise it. Sauces are made from entirely separate ingredients and should not be confused with gravies which come from the liquid residue in the pan after the joint or the vegetable has been cooked.

There are only a few basic sauce recipes and from those all the others stem. Some cooks still look upon a white sauce as an expedient rather than as an end in itself. But as much care should go into the making of a good plain white sauce as into a complicated recipe for a pudding garnish.

One rarely hears the word *thickening* any more. That method was never very successful anyway.

Nowadays the beginning of a white sauce is the melted butter in the top of the double boiler, for the *roux*. The double boiler, the perfectly blended *roux,* the pre-heated liquid which prevents lumping, the right seasoning—that's all one needs to make it. If you can't make a white sauce well, you can't make a good onion sauce. Don't blame the onion if it goes wrong.

A few sauces have been included in this book so that I could present together the means of making all the dishes suggested. The combinations, exactions, and flavors in the art of sauce making are endless. A family's prejudices and its allergies are sometimes the incentive which sends a cook adventuring in this wide field. What if Fame is lurking around your double boiler?

Remember that shallots (see page 8), because milder, are ideal as an onion-flavoring ingredient for most sauces. If shallots are easily obtained in your region, it is permissible to substitute them for any of the tablespoons of minced onions in the following pages.

For those sauces which do not have a cream base, it is better to use an onion.

BARBECUE SAUCE FOR MEATS

2 tbsp. butter
2 tbsp. brown sugar
4 tbsp. vinegar
1 cup tomatoes
1 onion, chopped
1 tsp. Worcestershire sauce
½ cup chopped celery
½ cup water
  pinch cayenne pepper
1 tsp. chili powder
½ tsp. mustard

Combine dry ingredients and blend together. Sauté onion and celery in the butter and add seasonings. Simmer until onion is soft, at least 20 minutes. Use for basting broiling chickens or roast.

CORN RELISH

12 ears sweet corn
 1 quart ripe tomatoes
 3 onions
 1 quart chopped celery
 2 cups sugar

    1 tbsp. mustard seed
    2 tbsp. celery seed
    2 tbsp. salt
    6 green peppers
    1 quart vinegar

Cut corn from cob. Chop onions and peppers. Combine with other ingredients and cook half an hour, stirring to prevent burning. Quantity: About 6 pints.

CHILI SAUCE

    11 lbs. ripe tomatoes
     4 green peppers
     4 sweet red peppers
     1 lb. onions
     4 lbs. green tomatoes
     6 tbsp. salt
     1 tbsp. celery seed
     3 cups sugar
     1 tbsp. ginger
    ½ tsp. cayenne pepper
     1 tsp. cinnamon
     1 tbsp. dry mustard
     2 cups vinegar

Grind green tomatoes in food chopper and the onions, and chop red tomatoes fine. Drain excess juice from both if you don't want to take time to cook the mixture down. Cook everything together until thick, stirring almost constantly.

This recipe has an entirely different flavor if made with all red tomatoes and ripe peppers instead of including the green ones.

DILL SAUCE—CREAM BASE

     1 medium sized Spanish onion
    1½ tbsp. butter
    ½ tbsp. flour

1 cup milk
⅛ tsp. combined nutmeg, salt, and black pepper
1 tsp. chopped fresh dill or
1½ powdered dill

Mince onion, and cook in the butter until the onion is clear but not brown. Dust with the flour and blend. Meantime the milk should have been scalded. Stir into the onions and flour and after it is thoroughly cooked, stirring constantly, for about five minutes, add seasonings, reserving the dill for the last minute before serving, cooking about three minutes longer.

This is good with cold meat.

DILL SAUCE—SOUR CREAM BASE

1 cup thick sour cream
1 tbsp. herb salad vinegar
1 tbsp. grated onion (Italian red for stronger flavor)
1 tsp. sugar
⅛ tsp. salt, pepper combined
1 scant tsp. minced fresh dill or 1½ powdered

Blend onion, vinegar and seasonings and fold into the cream. Let flavor permeate well before serving. Good with fish.

ENGLISH BREAD SAUCE

1 cup sweet milk
2 tbsp. shallots, grated
2 cloves
¾ cup soft bread crumbs
salt and pepper, q.s.
3 tbsp. sweet cream

Combine milk, onion and cloves and bring to a boil. Strain, add bread crumbs and cook, stirring constantly until the mixture is like heavy cream. Simmer for about 15 minutes. Season. Scald the cream, and add just before serving.

HORSERADISH WITH COTTAGE CHEESE

    ½ cup heavy cream
    ½ cup cottage cheese
    1½ tsp. prepared mustard
    5 tbsp. grated horseradish
    3 tbsp. chopped chives
    2 tsp. sugar
      salt to taste

Sieve the cottage cheese. Whip the cream. Combine and stir in the seasonings. Chill and serve.

If fresh horseradish is not available, use the bottled, adding another teaspoon of sugar to counteract the sharp taste of the vinegar on the horseradish.

HOLLANDAISE SAUCE FOR LEEKS
OR SCALLIONS

    ½ cup butter
    1 tbsp. lemon juice
    2 egg yolks
      pinch salt
      pinch cayenne

Make this in a double boiler. Have the water boiling in the base before beginning.

Melt one-third of the butter in the top and add the lemon juice and egg yolks. Beat with a fork or small wire whisk. It will foam and begin to thicken and, as it does, add another third of the butter and cook. Add the third remaining piece of butter and cook until thick.

Season after taking from fire.

Your other pair of hands will have cooked the leeks or the scallions and laid them on a platter to keep hot while waiting for the sauce.

LEMON JUICE AND ONION DRESSING

½ cup lemon juice
½ cup oil (salad or olive)
1 tsp. salt
1 tsp. paprika
2 tbsp. sugar
2 tsp. onion juice
2 tsp. chopped chives

MASON JAR DRESSING

This recipe is like an add-a-pearl necklace. Some cooks will want to add one ingredient, some another. But in the end it will be right for the purpose, as decorative as a necklace and almost as satisfying.

1 can condensed tomato soup
¾ cup herb salad vinegar
1 tsp. salt
½ tsp. paprika
½ tsp. pepper
1 tsp. onion juice
1 tbsp. mustard
1½ cups oil, salad or olive
½ cup sugar

Combine dry ingredients separately and liquid ingredients separately. Moisten the dry with a little of the liquid, then pour all together in a quart fruit jar and SHAKE.

Change the onion juice to 1 tbsp. if you do not want a clove of garlic in the SHAKE. And always shake before serving. You won't have to, many times. It doesn't last long.

Worcestershire sauce is a pearl to add. And a little of the liquid from dill pickles, another.

OLIVE SAUCE

2 tbsp. butter
2 tbsp. flour
1 cup stock
½ tsp. salt
½ tsp. paprika
1 tbsp. lemon juice
1 tsp. sugar
2 tbsp. minced onion
½ can tomato sauce
1 small bottle stuffed olives
or
1 small can ripe olives

Make a sauce by browning butter and flour before cooking into a *roux,* and thin with the stock. Chop the olives and add to the tomato sauce, with seasonings, lemon juice, and onion. When blended, combine with the brown sauce and cook ten minutes over low heat, stirring a little to prevent sugar burn.

Serve hot with roast veal instead of gravy, or with a mild fish.

MINT AND ONION DRESSING

1 bunch fresh mint
1 white onion
1 green pepper
¼ cup French dressing made with lemon juice
salt to taste

Chop mint leaves (not stems) and the onion, and add the chopped pepper, after removing seeds and ribs. Toss with the dressing, chill and serve with cold lamb.

MUSTARD BUTTER

1 tsp. dry mustard
6 tbsp. melted butter

4 tsp. sugar
½ tsp. salt
½ tsp. paprika

Dress small boiled onions with this sauce and serve hot.

ONION BUTTER FOR STEAK

1 thick slice Bermuda onion
4 tbsp. minced parsley
4 tbsp. butter
1 tsp. Worcestershire sauce
½ tsp. salt
¼ tsp. dry mustard
½ tsp. black pepper

Grate onion and mix to a smooth paste with other ingredients. Spread over steak after broiling and the heat of the meat will melt the butter base of the sauce.

ONION SAUCE FOR CAULIFLOWER

1 cup fine bread crumbs
⅓ cup butter
¼ cup toasted almonds, cut fine
4 tbsp. minced onion
  salt to taste, if any necessary

Sauté onion in some of the butter until tender. Combine with other ingredients and pour over top of a cauliflower head that has been cooked whole.

SAGE SAUCE

1 Spanish onion
1 tbsp. butter
¼ tsp. salt
⅛ tsp. black pepper

pinch dried sage
½ cup coffee cream
½ cup chicken stock (or canned broth)
2 tbsp. bread crumbs

Mince onion, cook in butter, combine dry seasonings and bread crumbs, and blend. Combine liquids and pour on onions. Cook until thickened, stirring constantly.

This is good with baked fish.

LOUISIANA SAUCE FOR SHRIMP

¾ pint stiff mayonnaise
5 tbsp. tomato catsup
1 tbsp. Worcestershire
dash of red pepper sauce
1 tsp. horseradish mustard or plain mustard
salt as desired
3 garlic buds
3 small shallots (fresh ones and add tops) if available; or
1 tbsp. anchovy paste and check salt

Mash the garlic buds in a bowl, or cut one and rub the bowl with it. Remove. Chop shallots, or blend anchovy paste into mayonnaise with other ingredients.

This is a sauce for boiled shrimp, crab meat, lobster or crayfish. These ingredients make 1 pint and it keeps indefinitely in the refrigerator in a covered jar.

SOUR CREAM DRESSING FOR COLE SLAW

½ cup sour cream
1½ tsp. salt
¼ cup cider or herb salad vinegar
2 tbsp. sugar
½ tsp. dry mustard
2 scallions, chopped fine

Combine vinegar and seasonings, blend with cream and toss shredded cabbage in it, allowing to stand before serving for flavor to permeate.

SPANISH SAUCE

2 tbsp. olive oil
2 Spanish onions
1 large sweet green pepper
1 cup canned tomatoes
1 tsp. salt
½ tsp. paprika

Cook minced onions and chopped pepper in hot oil until they begin to brown. Add tomatoes and seasonings and stir until blended and thick.

Serve with fried eggplant.

VINAIGRETTE

½ cup salad oil
¼ cup herb salad vinegar
1 tsp. chopped chives
1 tsp. chopped parsley
1 hard-cooked egg yolk
1 tsp. capers
   salt and pepper, q.s.
   other herbs optional with this, but necessary
   if plain vinegar is used

Mash the egg yolk in a bowl, moisten with a little of the oil. Blend the condiments and add to the egg until the dressing is thoroughly compounded. Beat again before serving.

WHITE SAUCE

This is best made in a double boiler. It prevents burning and after the sauce is made, if it is to be used at once, it is easier to keep it hot.

Be sure to follow the recipe exactly in which white sauce appears. The full amount of butter called for should be used. If not, it lumps. Let the butter melt completely before adding the flour and let the *roux* cook three minutes or so before adding the milk. If the milk is pre-heated it will make a smoother sauce. Stir constantly while blending the milk.

> 2 tbsp. butter
> 2 tbsp. flour
> 1 cup milk
> ½ tsp. salt
> pinch of pepper

This makes one cup white sauce.

SAUCE VELOUTE

This is made in the same way as white sauce, using veal stock instead of milk for liquid.

SAUCE SOUBISE

A white or a brown sauce containing onions. Named for a royal onion enthusiast and *chef extraordinaire* to a French king.

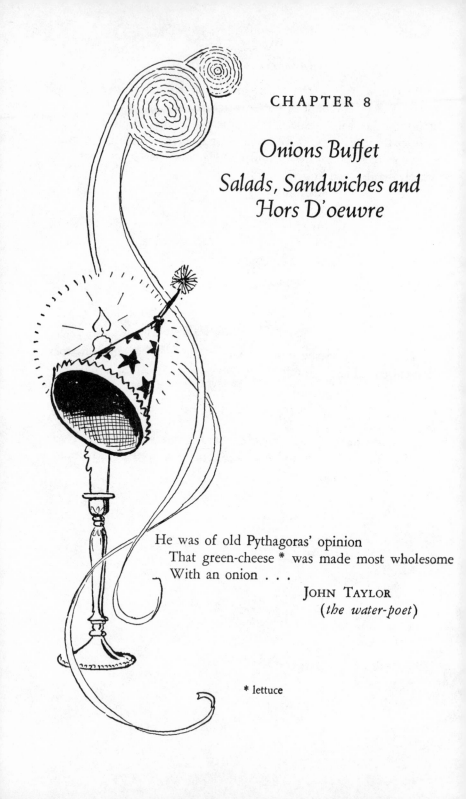

CHAPTER 8

Onions Buffet
Salads, Sandwiches and
Hors D'oeuvre

He was of old Pythagoras' opinion
That green-cheese * was made most wholesome
With an onion . . .

JOHN TAYLOR
(*the water-poet*)

* lettuce

This could have been called a party chapter. But I am a firm believer in making the family the party of the first part and of the first taste. If they like a thing, company folks will, too. It's as sure as the equinox. After trying it on the family, something new can be served with poise and aplomb and nobody knowing it's perhaps only the second time of performing.

It would be impossible to list the many ways in which it is possible to perk up the flavor of accessory food with a bit of chopped or minced onion, chives, or a pod of garlic. I should feel like Scheherazade truly if I were to attempt it. But you will find in these salads, sandwiches, and hors d'oeuvre some of the thousand and one that I like.

SALADS

AVOCADO WITH CRAB LOUIS
1 lb. crab meat, picked from shell
½ avocado per person
Louisiana shrimp sauce (see page 83)

Chill and serve
Onions with avocado suggest soup or a cold appetizer, crunchy

rolls and something wonderful in the way of desserts, plus hot coffee of course, to make a company meal, any day, any region.

AVOCADO WITH PEARL ONIONS

½ avocado per person
lettuce to serve it on
pearl onions to serve in the avocado
lemon French dressing to serve on the pearls

Lemon juice is a good antidote for the black look of an avocado after it has been cut, while waiting to be served. Brush with the juice over all the cut surface, and salt slightly, before filling with mixture of choice.

AVOCADO WITH CHICKEN SALAD

Marinate pieces of white meat of chicken in Spanish sauce for a half hour before making up into salad. Fill avocado halves and serve with fresh watercress and lettuce.

AVOCADO SALAD RING

1 envelope unflavored gelatin
¼ cup cold water
1 cup boiling water
2 tbsp. lemon juice
1 tsp. sugar
½ cup sour cream
½ cup any good commercial mayonnaise
2 medium sized avocados
4 tbsp. grated onion
1 tsp. salt

Soak the gelatin in the cold water. Dissolve with the boiling water. Stir in 1 tbsp. lemon juice and the sugar, and when clear, chill in refrigerator until it begins to set.

Rub the avocados through a fine sieve to make one cup of pulp. Add the second tbsp. lemon juice, and grated onion and combine with the cream and mayonnaise. Check seasoning, for salt, and add more if necessary.

Combine with the chilled gelatin.

Rinse a ring mold with cold water, and pack the mixture away to set. Cover mold with paraffin paper, fastening with a rubber band around the edge of the mold.

This is a decorative dish for any use. Serve with cold meat, Katie's Casserole, and chilled peaches, home style, for a bridge luncheon.

BEET AND ONION SALAD

Use small whole beets, marinated in lemon dressing
1 small white onion cut into rings and rolled in chopped parsley

Serve in crisp cups of Boston lettuce.

GREEN BEAN SALAD

2 cups cooked green beans
4 strips bacon
2 sweet onions
1 cup cold cooked potato, diced
2 tbsp. minced pimiento
  seasonings

Cook bacon until crisp enough to crumble. Combine with beans and potato and marinate in French dressing. Top with rings of onion, rolled in chopped parsley.

JELLIED SUMMER SALAD

1 tbsp. plain gelatin
¼ cup cold water

1 cup tomato juice
3 tbsp. herb salad vinegar
1 tbsp. lemon juice
4 level tbsp. sugar
½ tsp. salt
⅛ tsp. black pepper
1 small white onion, minced
1½ cups cooked vegetables (carrots, peas, celery, green or baby limas, etc.) or
1 can Vegetable Mix, in which each kind is separated from the next by paper
1 small bottle stuffed olives

Soften the gelatin in the cold water. Heat the tomato juice, vinegar, lemon juice, and minced onion and add dry seasonings. Combine with the gelatin and cool.

Rinse a ring mold in cold water. Cut the olives in two and make a ring at the bottom of the mold, each cut side down and touching the next piece. Lay the vegetables in, mixed or in sections as you wish them to appear when unmolded, and as soon as the liquid begins to thicken, pour over the vegetables in the mold.

Serve with a bowl of mayonnaise set in the center of the unmolded ring or fill it with lettuce or watercress leaves for garnish, and pass the mayonnaise.

ONION AND CUCUMBER SALAD

1 Bermuda onion
1 cucumber
2 tbsp. milk
2 tbsp. heavy cream
1 carton cottage cheese
shredded lettuce. q.s. to four servings

Reduce thickness of cottage cheese with milk and cream.

Slice and crisp the onion in rings, 15 minutes in a bowl of ice water. Arrange cucumber slices on the shredded lettuce with onion rings on top. In center, mound the seasoned cheese and dust with paprika.

ORANGE AND ONION SALAD

1 red Italian onion
½ orange for each serving
water cress and lettuce

Slice onion and break into rings, crisp in ice water, and arrange on each plate with sections of orange, or sliced orange and serve with French dressing in which chopped chives have been marinated.

PEPPER AND CHEESE RINGS

Select a sweet green pepper with deeply indented scallops, three or four. Wash to remove garden dust that may have collected in the folds. Remove the top and clip out the inner membrane holding the seed cluster. Fill with the following mixture, packing it down firmly:

¼ lb. cheddar cheese
1 small Bermuda onion
2 tbsp. milk (more if necessary)

Mince the onion, mash the cheese and moisten it with the milk, blending until creamy, and add the onion.

Set the filled shell in the refrigerator to harden and when ready to serve, slice crosswise with a sharp knife. Dust with paprika or minced parsley and arrange on lettuce leaves for individual salads, or use as a garnish for a platter of cold meat. A little chopped pimiento may be added to the cheese mixture before filling, if desired.

POTATO SALAD

There are many variations with the same name, but "two things greater than all things are" in potato salad and they are, after the potatoes, the eggs and the onions. So, chill the potatoes thoroughly before mixing, if for a cold salad, or heat them as thoroughly for a hot one, and go on from there.

POTATO SALAD, HOT

5 medium size boiled potatoes
2 hard-cooked eggs
5 slices cooked bacon
2 small white onions, minced
1 egg
¼ cup herb salad vinegar
2 tsp. salt

Cut potatoes in slices into the salad bowl while still hot. Add chopped eggs, bacon and onion. Beat raw egg and pour over, tossing thoroughly. Heat vinegar and salt, add and marinate before serving. Keep hot.

POTATO SALAD, CHILLED

5 medium size boiled potatoes
  (1 for each person and one for the bowl)
½ cup thick mayonnaise
¼ cup thick sour cream
3 hard-cooked eggs
1 strip pimiento chopped
½ medium sized cucumber, sliced
1 medium sized Bermuda onion or
½ a large Bermuda
  heart of one celery stalk, chopped
1 tbsp. green pepper, chopped (optional)
  seasonings
½ cup English walnuts, shelled

Some cooks will prefer crumbled bacon to the walnuts. Others will substitute a couple of crisp radishes, sliced, for the pimiento. If no fresh celery is available, use ¼ tsp. of celery seed.

Reserve four center slices from one of the eggs to garnish the top. Dust the yolk part with paprika and set a perfect walnut half on each.

Make the salad in time for flavors to blend thoroughly before serving. Arrange in a lettuce lined bowl, or in lettuce cups surrounding the picnic ham.

SALAD EGGS

Hard cook uniform sized eggs, one or two to a person and, when they are cool, shell and cut in half lengthwise, and scoop out the yolks into a bowl. Set the white halves aside on a plate ready for stuffing.

Mash the yolks with chosen seasonings, to taste. Plenty of salt, which egg yolks need, and then pepper, mustard, a pinch of curry powder, minced onion, etc., and moisten with Philadelphia cream cheese, cottage cheese, mayonnaise, boiled salad dressing or plain cream. When the mixture is fluffy and easy to work with, fill the halves, heaping up the center, using a spoon or icing tube, and garnish with chopped chives or fresh parsley, or one small parsley leaf, whole.

How to Hard Cook Eggs

There are a few simple things to remember about preparing hard-cooked eggs for salads.

Eggs are apt to crack during cooking if they are taken from the refrigerator and put on the stove at once. Let the eggs stand out in the room for about a half hour before cooking.

If the eggs are to be stuffed for garnish on the salad platter or to make a separate dish, it is much easier to prepare them if the yolks are centered. This can be managed by rolling them about gently with a spoon in the hot water while they are cooking.

Take the eggs out of the water as soon as they are done, and crack the shells to let the steam out. This provides also for the escape of the sulfur in the yolk and prevents a black ring forming around the outside of the yolk.

Chill in cold water.

TOMATO AND ONION SALAD

Slice 1 onion and 2 tomatoes very thin and marinate in herb vinegar until ready to serve. Arrange in 4 lettuce cups, after draining, on a large plate centered with a bowl of mayonnaise that has been sprinkled with chopped chives.

TOMATO SALAD WITH HAM

4 ripe tomatoes
1 pkg. cottage cheese
2 tbsp. minced ham
2 tbsp. mayonnaise
2 tbsp. onion, chopped fine
3 tbsp. green pepper, chopped fine
1 tsp. salt
pinch black pepper

Make tomato shells and turn upside down to drain.

Combine meat and mayonnaise and after salting the shells, coat with the mixture and fill center with the drained tomato pulp, the cheese, onion, pepper and seasonings, well blended.

Dust top with paprika. Serve with French dressing.

FROZEN TOMATO SALAD

1 tbsp. sugar
1 tsp. salt
⅛ tsp. curry powder
1 cup tomato pulp
1 cup shredded celery
4 tbsp. chopped onion
1 cup mayonnaise
½ cup sour cream
1 cup cottage cheese

Combine dry ingredients and moisten with tomato juice. Add to tomatoes. Whip the sour cream and blend with the cheese and mayonnaise. Fold in the seasoned tomato pulp, the celery and onion and pack in refrigerator pans to set, for five hours. Serve in squares on lettuce.

SANDWICHES

Mayonnaise is a good beginning spread for a meat sandwich. It is already soft and already flavored—two advantages. Whole grain breads are good for cheese and onions, and chives go with cheese on white bread, date bread, wheat or rye.

ONION AND CUCUMBER SANDWICH

Slice raw cucumber very thin. Peel and slice small sweet white onions in equal number. Lay between slices of rye bread which have been spread with mayonnaise. Season with salt and pepper.

TOAST CORNUCOPIAS

Slice fresh bread very thin, and cut off crusts. Toast the small squares lightly, in the oven under the broiler flame. Roll into a cornucopia quickly after brushing with butter and when shape is set, fill with spread previously prepared, with either a chicken liver base or chopped mayonnaise eggs.

BACON AND FRIED ONION SANDWICH

Fry onions as for steak. Prepare bacon strips and fry well done so they will crumble easily. Add the crumbs to the butter or mayonnaise spread for the bread. Drain fat off the onions before spreading on the bread.

HAMBURGER SANDWICHES

Fried onions are good in a hamburger bun, too, if no minced onion has been mixed with the hamburger when it was prepared for browning. Remember that hamburger patties for sandwiches should be made quite thin, so the sandwich isn't too thick. They can be broiled more quickly too, if they are thin.

BAKED BEAN SANDWICH

1 tbsp. cream
1 cup canned baked beans
2 tbsp. chili sauce
2 tbsp. chopped onion
season to taste

Mash beans with a fork and smooth with the cream. Combine with the other ingredients and spread.

HOT ONION SANDWICH

Make filling for Filled Onion Tarts on page 71. Toast rounds of bread on one side only. Spread untoasted side with the pie filling, run under the broiler until browned, and serve hot.

CHICKEN LIVER SANDWICH

3 cooked chicken livers
1 hard-cooked egg
4 tbsp. butter
2 tbsp. cream
1/4 tsp. salt
1/8 tsp. black pepper
1 small onion

Peel onion and slice very thin. Fry in the melted butter until light brown. Chop livers and egg fine, combine with milk and seasonings, and add to the onions. Cook 5 minutes more, stirring until well blended.

Use this spread for a hot toasted sandwich. Or mold and use cold.

EAST INDIA CURRY SPREAD

2 oz. strong cheese, grated
2 tbsp. butter
1 tsp. curry powder
2 eggs
1 tbsp. onion juice
  pinch cayenne
  salt, q.s.

Melt butter in saucepan. When hot, stir in curry powder and fry lightly. Add cheese, salt, pepper, and last of all the eggs which have been slightly beaten, and cook to consistency of scrambled eggs. Fill sandwiches.

FROSTED SANDWICH LOAF

This is a versatile recipe. It can be a main dish for a high tea on Sunday night, or for a luncheon, with a dessert.

2 packages Philadelphia cream cheese
1 unsliced loaf of white bread
3 bowls of sandwich fillings

Cut off all the crusts of the loaf so that you have a smooth, even oblong. Slice lengthwise with a sharp knife, so that you have three or four long thin slices. Spread the upper side of the bottom layer with butter and the under side of the next layer and fill with the first mixture, which should be firm enough to stay in place. Spread thinly, so that sandwich will not tower when it is completed.

Repeat and press down gently with the hands until you are sure that the sandwich will stay together. Ice top and sides with the cream cheese which has been mashed with a little milk to make it spread easily. A spatula is good for the spreading. Chill in refrigerator until ready to serve. Make early so flavors will blend.

Garnish with parsley, sliced stuffed olives or chopped chives.

Fillings: There are many possibilities. Two that go well together are salad eggs (whites and seasoned yolks mashed together), and a sharp yellow cheese, moistened with milk and creamed until it will spread. Or, flavor the eggs with mustard or curry powder and combine the onion with the cheese. Tuna fish salad, if minced fine, is a good layer.

ONE BERMUDA, COMING UP

Cut bread in rounds with a biscuit or doughnut cutter.

½ lb. snappy cheese
1 Bermuda onion
2 long strips bacon

Put these through a meat grinder and mix thoroughly. Spread on the bread rounds and run under broiler just before serving.

ONION AND CARAWAY SPREAD

½ lb. American cheddar cheese
3 tbsp. coffee cream
1 tbsp. grated onion
½ tsp. caraway seeds
¼ tsp. salt
pinch pepper

Cut up the cheese, and moisten with the cream. Season with onion and combine with caraway. Blend with the cheese and let stand a while before use.

ONION CLUB SANDWICH

Spread rye or whole wheat bread with sliced Bermuda or Italian onion, thin slices of ham and cheese, water cress and bacon butter.

ONION AND MUSHROOM CANAPÉ

1 Spanish onion, or
2 small white

    1 lb. fresh mushrooms
    seasoning
    toast rounds
    2 tbsp. butter

Wash and peel the mushrooms and chop. Peel onion and chop. Sauté in the melted butter and season. Bind with a little flour, and when thick spread on toast rounds and brown under broiler.

ONION AND PEPPER SANDWICH

    1 pkg. Philadelphia cream cheese
    1 tbsp. scraped Spanish onion
    2 tbsp. chopped sweet green pepper
    3 cups boiling water

Pour boiling water over the chopped mixture in a sieve. Mash cheese with a small amount of thin cream to spreading consistency. Add onion and pepper, season with salt and pepper to taste, and let stand in refrigerator an hour to blend before making sandwiches. Use whole wheat bread.

SCALLION CANAPE

Spread an oblong of soft bread with cream cheese. Cut a clean scallion as long as the width of the bread and roll as for jelly roll. Fasten edges with a little of the cheese and pack in waxed paper until ready to serve.

TOMATO CANAPÉ

    ½ cup boiled salad dressing
    ¼ cup cold milk
    1 tsp. unflavored gelatin
    2 tbsp. finely chopped onion
    2 tbsp. finely chopped green pepper

Dissolve gelatin in the milk over hot water. Add dressing, onion and pepper, and mold in small cups.

Toast thin slices of bread, cut in rounds, spread with soft butter and place on each a thin, drained slice of peeled tomato. Unmold gelatin cups, slice and place one on each canapé. Top each with a spoonful of whipped cream, dusted with fresh chopped parsley or paprika.

*VIENNA BREAD AND MUSTARD BUTTER

This is a variation of the garlic bread in a later chapter (see page 140).

Flavor softened butter with mustard, just enough to spike it well. Cut a loaf of Vienna bread on the bias in inch slices, not quite through to the bottom. Spread both sides of each cut with the prepared butter. Have ready enough slices of Bermuda onion, not too large across so they won't stick out of the loaf, to put between each gash in the bread. Push the loaf together and tie a string around to hold it. Cover top with paper thin slices of sharp cheese. Run under the broiler flame until the cheese melts down into the bread. Clip apart with kitchen scissors to serve.

HORS D'OEUVRE

"Eat no onions nor garlic, for we
are to utter sweet breath."
Midsummer Night's Dream

Too many hostesses are afraid to serve hors d'oeuvre with onion and garlic. They forget that if all their guests are eating the same thing, nobody will notice the taint . . . and there is always parsley. A crystal bowl with a few ice cubes and water and small whole leaves of parsley afloat might even be a good conversation piece. One canapé, one sprig.

But the parsley idea needn't be reserved for parties. There is a place I know, quite a good place for getting hamburgers, be-

* This comes in a long crusty loaf, that is fluffy inside, another version is the hard roll restaurants serve.

cause they put honest-to-goodness beef in them and add Bermuda in raw rings. And at the very end of the cashier's counter, the last thing before you reach the door, and after you have paid, is a parsley bowl. The free bouquet is a good investment. It can't but add to the dividends when the word gets round.

DIP FOR PINEAPPLE

Add two tbsp. mayonnaise to Horseradish Sauce on page 79 and use as a dip for drained pineapple chunks.

DIPS FOR POTATO CHIPS

1. Moisten 1 package Philadelphia cream cheese with ¼ cup mayonnaise, ¼ tsp. Worcestershire sauce and a little cream. Beat to a fluff and pile up in a cut glass bowl.
2. Avocado dip. Season the pulp of one avocado with lemon juice, Worcestershire sauce, a pinch of curry powder, some garlic salt, and a little plain white table salt.
3. Sour cream, whipped very stiff, salted and *full* enough of chopped chives to look a little green. There will be parsley lurking about.

DIP FOR TUNA FISH

Get a can of the bite-size tuna, separate and drain. Roll in minced chives and arrange on the tray with cottage cheese that has been stiffened with sweet whipped cream. And salted, too.

A DIP PADDLE

Cut outside blossoms (because they are the largest) from a head of cauliflower, leaving as much stem on as possible, and slice thinly through the middle. Serve as paddles for the avocado mixture.

BROILED MUSHROOMS

One per person to garnish a dinner plate.
As many as you wish, for a buffet spread.
Q.S. to Twelve, here:

      ½ cup fine bread crumbs
      4 tbsp. butter
      1 tbsp. grated onion
      ½ tbsp. chopped parsley
      ½ tsp. chopped chives
      ½ tsp. salt
        pinch nutmeg
      4 tbsp. grated cheese

Peel mushroom caps and sauté in butter. Remove and set aside.
Peel and chop stems fine, sauté in butter, add bread crumbs and
seasonings, blend and cook. Fill caps, top with cheese and run
under broiler.

One may substitute crumbled bacon for the cheese.

GARLIC OLIVES

Buy green olives stuffed with celery, in a garlic brine. Drain.
Wrap each olive with a piece of bacon just long enough to lap
and secure with toothpick. Lay on broiler rack with toothpick at
the horizontal to prevent its burning. Broil until the bacon is
brown and sizzling. Serve hot with canapés.

HORS D'OEUVRE EGGS

      4 hard-cooked eggs
      2 chicken livers, cooked
      2 tsp. grated onion
        paprika, salt and pepper to taste
      2 tbsp. cream

Cut each egg in four, lengthwise. Remove the yolks, and place
in a mixing bowl. Mash the livers with a fork until any remain-

ing membrane can be pulled away easily. Mince the eggs with a fork, add cream and onion and seasonings with the livers, and make a smooth filling for the whites. Fill with a narrow grapefruit spoon, or with an icing tube, and arrange on serving plate, with water cress. Dust a little paprika on top.

ONION PUFFS

These are bite size cream puff shells, filled with several different appetizers. For the puff paste, follow these directions:

      1 cup water
      ½ cup butter
      ¼ tsp. salt
      1 cup sifted all purpose flour
      4 eggs

Heat water, fat and salt to boiling. Simmer until fat has melted.

Reduce heat to lowest possible flame, and add flour all at once, stirring briskly until the mixture comes together in a mass in the center of the pan. Cut off heat.

Add eggs one at a time, beating after each addition until the mixture is stiff and glossy.

To bake the Onion Puffs, measure a scant teaspoonful of paste for each one, spacing about two inches apart on a lightly greased cookie sheet. Bake about half an hour in a hot oven. This amount makes four dozen cocktail shells. They should be browned and quite dry when done.

To fill, cut off the top with a sharp knife, add mixture, replacing the top.

Fillings: 1. Onion and mushroom canapé mixture.

2. Whipped cream, salted and seasoned with onion as for top of cream of pea soup.
3. Creamed onion, page 34.
4. Filling for the little pies, page 72.
5. Stiff sour cream with chives flavor.
6. Onion and chicken liver sandwich spread.

*PEARL ONIONS

Roll each one in finely chopped parsley and serve between black olives and rose-cut radishes on an hors d'oeuvre tray. These will disappear any time of day, with or without a toothpick.

SHRIMPS IN CELERY STALKS

Select a bunch of celery with wide stalks, preferably Pascal. Marinate small canned shrimp in onion-flavored mayonnaise and arrange in the cut lengths of celery, about three to a serving. Dust with paprika or chives.

STUFFED CELERY

          1 package Philadelphia cream cheese
       1½ tbsp. minced onion (any seasonal sort)
          1 tbsp. minced parsley, or
             sweet green pepper
       ¼ cup light cream
             salt, pepper, paprika

This will fill 20 celery sticks 3 or 4 inches long or it can be mounded on quartered hearts of celery, with the leaves left on.

STUFFED CUCUMBER

Choose a firm cucumber that is beginning to turn yellow at one end. Slice off blossom end and remove center with apple corer. Fill with mixture for stuffed celery, cover open end with wax paper and refrigerate. When ready to serve, slice crosswise with a very sharp knife so that the center stays with its slice, and arrange in a circle, with water cress, on a glass plate.

This can be done with a big dill pickle, too. Wipe it dry and proceed as above.

* These are the tiny pickles like white grapes that are sold in bottles.

TOMATO JUICE WITH ONION SALT

> 1 can tomato juice, No. 2 size
> 1 tbsp. sugar
> 3 or 4 whole cloves
> 1/4 tsp. onion salt
> 1 tsp. table salt
> 1/4 tsp. black pepper
> 1 tbsp. lemon juice
> 1/2 stick cinnamon or 1/4 tsp. powdered

Combine all ingredients and bring to boil over moderate flame. Chill and serve.

TOMATO JUICE WITH ONION

> 4 cups tomato juice (1 large can)
> 2 heaping tbsp. finely chopped onion
> 1 small bay leaf, broken in pieces
> 1/2 cup chopped celery (leaves and stalk)
> 1 tbsp. Worcestershire sauce
> 2 tbsp. vinegar
> 1 tsp. salt
> 1 tbsp. sugar
> dash red pepper
> 6 whole cloves (optional)

Simmer until onion and leaves are very soft and strain through a fine sieve. Add remaining ingredients (salt and a little sugar and the dash of red pepper). Add cloves only if a spicy flavor is desired.

CHAPTER 9

With Poultry, Meats, and Miscellany

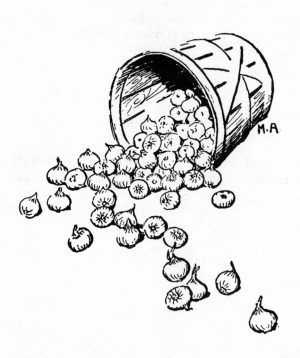

POULTRY

BARBECUED CHICKEN

Have chickens split for broiling. Rub with butter, but instead of basting them with seasoned butter during the broiling, as usual, use the Barbecue Sauce on page 76.

CHICKEN CURRY, AMERICAN

Prepare chicken as for creaming—stewed in broth and bones removed—cut in uniform pieces, both light and dark meat and heat in this curry gravy:

> ½ lb. fresh mushrooms
> 2 small white onions
> 1 small apple, or 1 small potato
> 4 tbsp. butter
> 2 tbsp. flour
> 1 cup chicken broth
> ¼ cup light cream
> ½ tsp. salt
> 1 tsp. curry powder
> 2 cups chicken meat

Wash and peel the mushrooms, cut caps in quarters and slice stems lengthwise in two. Peel onions and chop coarsely. Core the apple and slice, or dice the potato. Sauté onion in butter alone at first, then add the other solids. When soft, blend in flour, to which seasonings have been added, and the chicken broth. Cook until gravy has formed, and add the chicken. Check seasoning and thin with more cream if too thick, after adding amount called for.

CHICKEN PANCAKES

This could be called *chicken convenance,* almost, because the remainder from the bird with which the curry is made, can be used to make it.

           1½ cups ground cooked chicken
            1 cup milk
            2 tbsp. grated or minced fine onion
           ¼ cup butter
            2 cups flour (measured after sifting)
            4 tsp. baking powder
           ½ tsp. curry powder
            1 tsp. salt
           ⅛ tsp. nutmeg
              pinch cayenne

Sift dry ingredients together. Make a batter with the milk and fold in the onion, melted butter, and the chicken. Blend thoroughly, and bake on a hot griddle as one does any pancake.

Two served together with hot mushroom gravy might class as a special sort of shortcake.

CHICKEN PAPRIKA

Have the butcher joint a 3½-4 lb. fowl, Southern style, which means a wishbone piece, two pieces of breast and thighs and drumsticks cut apart, back split and two pieces of neck.

Reserve giblets and the two neck pieces for stewing separately to make the base of a casserole dish.

Go over the rest of the pieces carefully for feathers and blemishes, wash in cold water to work upon and in one last rinse of hot water, and wipe the chicken dry.

           ¼ lb. fresh mushrooms
            2 Spanish onions

4 tbsp. butter
1 cup sour cream
2 cups water
1 tsp. salt
1 tbsp. paprika

Mince onions and sauté in the butter until light brown, wash and slice mushrooms, and add to the onion, with seasonings, and the water. When it bubbles, lay the pieces of chicken in the pan, cover and simmer until it is tender.

Remove the chicken to a hot platter and keep hot. Add sour cream to the remaining liquid, thoroughly blend and heat through, and pour over the chicken.

Garnish with chopped parsley if desired.

FLAVORING SUGGESTIONS FOR POULTRY

SHALLOTS are splendid for flavoring broilers or young chickens that are to be roasted. Make a mixture of the following:

2 tbsp. finely chopped parsley
1 tbsp. minced shallot
1 tbsp. butter or olive oil
rosemary (optional)
chives, to taste

Push this beneath the skin on both sides of the breastbone, over the breast and down the sides, but don't break the skin. The pleasant blending of these flavors will cook through the bird and make a better cold slice, if there is any left to chill.

ONION SALT. Rub the inside of a small roasting chicken with this, as well as with table salt. The onion flavor will not be pronounced, but the chicken flavor will be enhanced.

ONION IN GAME DUCK. None of the authorities seem to feel that there is any help for a duck that has fed on fish, except to bury it, possibly; but if the duck is only a little wild, roast it with an onion tucked away in the middle, instead of *stuffing*.

Two Bermudas in a Goose. Instead of the usual seasoned bread dressing, salt a goose thoroughly inside and stow away two peeled Bermuda onions that have been slightly parboiled. That just gives them a little start. By the time the goose is done it will be flavored with onion and the onions with goose—a fair trade. A hostess I know did this and the men guests began bidding with each other for the Bermudas. That was before conversation pieces were made so much of, but she had them talking with no trouble.

MEATS

BEEF STEW

Never allow a stew to come to full boil. Simmer it.

Have the butcher cube for you 1½ lbs. stewing beef, and break the bones, for the sake of the marrow value.

Chop red Spanish onions to make one cup and sauté in melted beef fat. Sear the cubes of meat, after removing the onions.

Add water to cover, to the meat, in a large kettle, season and simmer one-half hour per pound of meat. Add vegetables of choice a half hour before the meat is done. Variety of vegetables is the cook's choice. There wouldn't be any turnips in mine. If whole small onions are to be used, let them cook at least twenty minutes before the other things are added.

CREAMED DRIED BEEF

¼ lb. dried beef
2 tbsp. melted beef fat
2 tbsp. minced onion
1¼ cups white sauce, or Sauce Veloute
¼ tsp. condiment sauce
nutmeg

Shred the beef, cover with cold water, and bring to a boil to reduce the salt content.

Heat the fat and stir in the drained beef, cooking over low heat for five minutes. Remove and keep hot.

Sauté the onion in the same pan, until it begins to turn brown. Drain the onions on a paper towel.

Heat the sauce, add seasonings, and fold in the beef and the onions.

Refer to shortcakes, page 62.

HAMBURGER

For hamburger meat prepared at home, run an onion through the grinder after all the meat has been ground. Add seasonings.

A mixture for a hamburger meat loaf calls for the following:

    1¼ lbs. chuck and pork combined, about 3-1
    ½ a large Bermuda onion (1 cup, chopped)
    1 slice soft white bread
    ½ can tomato soup (reserving 4 tbsp. for top)
    1 egg
    2 tbsp. green pepper minced
    1 tbsp. fat (butter or chicken fat)
    1 tsp. salt
      black pepper
      dash paprika
    1 tsp. sugar

To bake, pack in a greased ring mold. Spread crushed corn flakes scantily on top, and dot here and there with the soup set aside for the purpose. Serve with creamed potatoes in the center of the unmolded ring.

Or, make the mixture without the onions and serve with creamed onions in the center of the unmolded ring.

GREEN PEPPERS STUFFED WITH HAMBURGER

    2 large green peppers
    1 can hamburger patties
    ¼ cup cooked celery
    ½ cup cooked rice
        or
    1 cup coarse bread crumbs

Wash peppers, smooth stem end so it will stand up in the baking pan, cut peppers in two crosswise, and clip out membrane holding seeds.

Heat the patties in their own fat, and mash before combining with the celery and the crumbs (or rice). The patties are already onion flavored. Fill the pepper shells which have been parboiled in salted water, and top with crushed potato chips. Bake until peppers are tender.

HAM SOUFFLÉ

2 cups medium white sauce
⅓ cup grated cheese (American)
¾ cup minced celery
1½ tbsp. minced pimiento
1 cup cooked mushrooms
¾ cup cold boiled ham (chopped)
4 eggs, separated
¾ tsp. curry powder
2 tbsp. grated onion

To the white sauce add everything except whites of egg; be sure yolks are well beaten. Fold in stiff whites last. Turn all into a greased casserole and set in pan of hot water. Bake in moderate oven (350°) about 35 minutes or until nicely browned. Serves four.

JELLIED VEAL

Ask the butcher for a knuckle of veal to jelly. He will chop the bone open for you. The bone and meat, about three pounds, should be cooked with the usual ingredients for a stew. A good *bouquet garni* is as follows:

1 bay leaf
1 celery stalk and leaves
parsley
2 whole cloves

1 tbsp. salt
1 large chopped onion
1 clove garlic
1 tsp. black pepper

Assemble the *bouquet*, add to veal in a large kettle with water to cover and cook until the meat is tender to a fork, about three quarters of an hour.

Cool and strain the meat out of the broth, discarding the remains of the seasoning.

For a molded loaf, cut the meat in small cubes. This is preferable to mincing in a meat grinder. Kitchen scissors make the best cubes.

Measure two cups of stock. Dissolve one envelope of gelatin in ¼ cup cold water. Reheat the stock and add the dissolved gelatin and two tbsp. lemon juice. Pour over the cubed veal in the mold—a ring mold is good for this purpose.

There are many possible variations for this mold—peas, pimiento, tender cooked green beans, hard-cooked eggs in slices, stuffed olives, etc. Unmold when chilled, as for any jelly.

LAMB ELISABETH

4 lamb steaks, 1¼ inches thick, or
4 thick chops cut from leg of lamb
1 cup white onions chopped fine
1 cup minced fresh parsley
2 level tbsp. flour
  salt and pepper, q.s.

Wipe lamb with a damp cloth and arrange in a deep baking dish, two chops to a layer. Combine parsley and onions. Sprinkle each layer with seasoning and one tbsp. flour. Spread half of the parsley and onion mixture on each. Almost cover with domestic sauterne. Bake slowly about two hours.

Note: No fat is required in preparing this dish because the added liquids and flour make a gravy.

PORK CHOPS WITH BREAD DRESSING

Sear four chops until juices are sealed. Cover tightly and cook slowly until half done.

Prepare onion and bread dressing in the following proportions and pile one fourth of it on each chop. Bake uncovered until dressing is thoroughly browned.

> 4 medium sized white onions
> 4 tbsp. butter
> 1½ cups soft bread crumbs
> ½ tsp. salt
> ⅛ tsp. pepper
> 2 tbsp. parsley, chopped
> pinch sage
> 2 tbsp. water
> 1 egg well beaten

Chop onions, sauté in butter, soften crumbs with water, and combine with seasonings, folding in cooked onions with beaten egg.

SWEETBREADS

> 2 pairs sweetbreads
> 3 tbsp. butter
> 3 mushrooms
> ½ tsp. minced chives
> 1 shallot, minced
> 2 egg yolks
> ¼ tsp. lemon juice
> 2 tbsp. cream
> salt and pepper

Parboil sweetbreads, with a little lemon juice in the water to keep them white. Let stand in ice water for a half hour before removing the tubes and membranes. Drain and dry and cut into cubes or thick slices.

Peel and cut mushrooms in eighths. Sauté with sweetbreads in the butter, the sweetbreads a little longer, in all about ten minutes. Add shallot, chives and seasoning and cook another ten minutes while preparing the egg, cream and lemon juice mixture. Cook until thick and pour over sweetbreads. Serve with rice.

MISCELLANY

ONION IN RAREBIT

2 eggs
¼ cup chopped yellow onions
2 tbsp. melted butter
½ can tomato soup
¾ cup milk
½ tsp. mustard
2 cups cheddar cheese, cut fine

Cook onion in butter until soft. Combine soup and milk and pour over onions. Add mustard and cheese and stir until cheese has melted. Blend the beaten eggs with a little of the hot soup before adding to first mixture; remove from fire immediately it thickens.

ONION OMELET

1½ egg per person ⎫
1 tbsp. milk   ⎪ Multiply
1 tsp. fat per egg ⎬ by
salt and pepper ⎭ Four
½ cup white onions to 6 eggs
or chopped scallions

Sauté the onions or the scallions before the curtain rises. Blend with other ingredients and divide the mixture in four for individual omelets. Cook over low heat or eggs will be tough.

Serve with creamed chicken or a thick cheese sauce (white sauce with melted cheese added).

ONIONS WITH NOODLES
(Lasagne)

        12 oz. wide noodles
        ¼ lb. onions (about 6 small white)
        ¼ lb. mushrooms
         1 carton cottage cheese
        ¼ lb. grated sharp cheese
        ⅛ lb. sliced American cheese
         4 tbsp. butter
         1 large tomato
           salt and pepper

Chop onions and sauté until golden in the butter. Add mushrooms and the tomato, cut in small pieces. Simmer for 15 to 20 minutes. Add cottage cheese, mixing well with the sauce.

Meantime the noodles have been boiling according to directions on the package. Drain and dry on paper towels. Place in a buttered baking dish on ring mold. Spread with the sauce, sprinkle some grated cheese on top, lay the sliced cheese on top of that, season, and repeat until all the noodles and sauce are used. Place baking pan in a shallow pan of water and bake for an hour in a moderate oven.

MACARONI MOUSSE

         1 cup macaroni, broken in pieces
        1½ cups hot milk
         1 cup soft bread crumbs
        ¼ cup melted butter
         1 pimiento, chopped
         1 tbsp. chopped parsley
         1 tbsp. rounded, chopped onion
         1 pkg. Kraft American cheese grated
         3 eggs, salt and pepper

Cook macaroni, blanch in cold water. Pour hot milk over

crumbs, add butter, pimiento, parsley, onion, cheese, seasoning. Add the well beaten eggs last. Pour mixture over macaroni, and bake in a slow oven (325°) for about an hour or until knife inserted comes out clean.

Serve with mushroom sauce.

CHAPTER 10

The Onion Abroad

Provence with her garlic scented smile.
KIPLING

The onion is at home in so many countries that *abroad* must now be interpreted loosely to mean *elsewhere,* from a given point. Great Britain draws from the West Indies, from the Canary Islands, and from Egypt to augment home harvests of onions. American markets receive annually in the spring the large shipments from Egypt, which add to the variety available to our cooks. Red ones and the sweet mild purple from Italy come to increase the bouquet. And an American grown onion, though it be called Spanish, is a foreigner in Rome or Athens.

Onions are an ingredient common to many national dishes and whether one asks for an *oignon* in France, a *cipolla* in Italy, a *piyaz* in India, or a *cebula* in Poland, it will be a brown, or a red, or a yellow, or a white lily bulb and it will be something good to eat.

ARMENIA

ARMENIAN LEEKS

        1 bunch leeks
        1 bunch celery
        2 cups chicken stock
     ½ cup butter
    1½ tbsp. lemon juice
        3 egg yolks

Clean leeks and celery. If leeks are large, cut in halves. Remove coarse outer stalks of celery and quarter or eighth the center. Cook in the broth until tender. Drain and remove to serving platter; keep warm while sauce is being prepared.

Sauce Reduce remaining broth to about ¾ of a cup. Melt the butter, and add the warmed lemon juice. Drop the egg yolks in another, warm pan, and stir in slowly 4 tbsp. of the hot broth, blend the butter and lemon juice with it, and then the rest of the broth. This is a thin sauce similar to hollandaise. Pour over the leeks and celery on the platter and serve.

SHISH KEBABS

The principle of a *Kebab* in any language, is a broil, accomplished quickly over a glowing bed of coals. Pieces of meat, lamb in Armenia, cut in cubes, are alternated with slices of onion and other vegetables on skewers, the whole highly seasoned and turned slowly over the fire until done, when the bits are slid off onto the serving plate. The trick is to begin and end with a piece of meat and to push the skewerful compactly together for best results.

In Russia the same dish is known as *Shasslik*.

Armenian and Russian lamb-and-onion grill have a cousin in India, called by the Muslims *Qabab,* and it has the same ingredients prepared somewhat differently. There the skewers are thick at the cooking end, and the ground meat, highly seasoned with onions and spices, is molded onto the steel. When it is thoroughly cooked, it slides off and has the appearance of a hollow wienie.

Adapted by hostesses in the United States, variations of mushroom caps, cubes of beef instead of lamb, little folded squares of bacon, chicken livers, even chunks of apple are used. In cutting the onions they should be quartered instead of diced or sliced, so that the skewer point has something to pierce. Reserve the centers for the chopped onion called for in *Barbecue Sauce,* to brush on before the broiling.

In New York City a famous restaurant provides one with all the elements of a *Kebab,* served from a *Flaming Sword* instead of a skewer by a waiter in eastern dress. It's picturesque, but the food is more than that. It doesn't need a sword.

BELGIUM

WATERZOIE
(Chicken Soup)

1 roasting chicken, about 3½ lbs.
2 tbsp. butter
2 Spanish onions
6 leeks (1 bunch)
1 large carrot
3 stalks from a bunch of celery
3 tbsp. chopped parsley
1 bay leaf
  pinch of thyme (optional)
4 whole cloves
  salt and pepper, q.s.
½ lemon

Clean the chicken and rub it with the lemon. Put the bird whole into a large kettle and cook in enough water to cover. When it begins to boil, skim away the brown scum that always rises. Stick the cloves in the peeled onions and drop in the kettle. Dice leeks, carrot, and celery and cook in the butter until tender; but do not brown. Combine the seasonings with these and add to the chicken. Cook until it is tender, adding water if necessary. Remove to platter and carve in large slices, taking out all bones, and put the slices in the tureen in which the soup will be served. Skim off any remaining fat from the stock, remove the bay leaf, check seasoning, and pour over the chicken with the vegetables. Garnish with more chopped celery and serve.

BULGARIA

MOUSAKA
(Eggplant)

This is a scallop of beef and eggplant. Mousaka is the Bulgarian word for eggplant.

    1 medium sized eggplant
    3 between sized onions
    3 tbsp. butter
    2 ripe tomatoes
    1 lb. ground beef
    ½ lb. ground pork
    ½ tsp. paprika
    1 tsp. nutmeg
      salt and pepper, q.s.

Cut the eggplant crosswise in thick slices and peel. Salt each and set aside for the meat mixture.

Peel and chop the onions and tomatoes and cook in the butter with the seasonings. When the onions begin to brown, add the meat and blend thoroughly (until it changes color).

Wash the salt off the eggplant slices and place in a casserole alternately with the cooked mixture, beginning and ending with the meat. Add a quarter cup of water to start steam and bake in a moderate oven until eggplant tests tender to fork.

CHINA

EGG FOO YONG

    10 eggs
     1 cup water
     1 cup shredded onion
     1 cup chicken, meat, or fish, finely chopped
     2 cups bean sprouts
       salt and pepper

Drain sprouts. Combine with meat and onion. Beat eggs with water and add. Cook in hot fat, three-quarters of a cupful at a time, in individual omelets.

Serve with *Chinese Gravy*. This is stock thickened with corn-starch and seasoned with soya sauce, salt and pepper.

DENMARK

DANISH MEAT BALLS

  2 inch-thick slices bread
1½ lbs. ground beef
  1 red onion, minced
  4 tbsp. tried-out beef fat
  ½ cup hot water
  ½ tsp. salt
  ⅛ tsp. pepper
  ¼ tsp. nutmeg
  1 bay leaf

Pour the water over the bread in a mixing bowl. Drain and crumble. Put the bay leaf in the remaining water and reserve. Combine meat, onion and seasonings with the bread, and form into balls. Dust with flour and brown in the melted fat. Pour over the bay leaf water and cook slowly ½ hour. Serve hot with rice or noodles.

FRANCE

VICHYSSOISE

1 medium sized onion
3 leeks or green onions
2 tbsp. butter
2 tbsp. flour
4 medium sized potatoes
2 quarts chicken broth
3 pints milk
1 cup heavy cream

¼ cup chopped chives
⅛ tsp. nutmeg
   salt

Peel and slice onions and leeks very thin. Sauté in butter until faintly browned. Blend in flour, keeping color light. Add pared potatoes and broth and cook 40 minutes or until potatoes are very soft. Force through sieve. Scald milk and combine with potato and leek purée. Chill until ready to serve (overnight is best). Strain again for velvety smoothness, check seasoning, combine with heavy cream and sprinkle chopped chives on each cupful. Serve very cold.

HUNGARY

We have come to think of paprika and onions and sour cream as essentially Hungarian, but an authority on Hungarian cooking now admits that it has been only within the last hundred years that paprika was introduced there by the Turks coming in from the east. But with that first hundred years out of the way it does seem that paprika might be said to belong completely.

MUSHROOMS IN SOUR CREAM is a dish that accents all three national ingredients:

1 lb. mushrooms
3 tbsp. butter
2 tbsp. flour, level
¾ cup sour cream
2 medium sized white onions
   salt, paprika, and parsley to taste

Wash and slice the mushrooms (if you are a mushroom washer). Peel and slice the onions and cook in the butter until a golden brown. Add the mushrooms and cook together. Season. When the juice seems completely soaked in, dredge with the flour, blend, and add the cream. Bring to the boil.

Serve with fried eggs or croutons. Serve, period, seems as good a direction as any. It tastes like a dream without benefit of eggs.

GULYAS
(Hungarian Goulash)

2 lbs. beef, loin preferred
3 medium sized Spanish onions
  or enough to make 1½ cups when peeled
  and sliced
4 small potatoes
3 tbsp. beef drippings
1 clove garlic (optional)
1 tsp. salt
½ tsp. caraway seed
1 tbsp. paprika
1 green sweet pepper (in place of green paprika)
1 cup tomato juice or strained canned tomatoes

Cut the beef into cubes. Brown with the onions in the fat, stirring occasionally to prevent scorching. Add salt, caraway, garlic, paprika, and tomato juice. After a half hour of cooking, add cubed potatoes and diced pepper. Broth or more tomato juice may be added if the liquid soaks up before the potatoes are soft.

INDIA

CURRIES

In India it is the custom to make one's own curry paste and powders. The commercial sort we buy in America loses strength. Also there are many combinations of ingredients for the various sorts of curry and tastes in the different Provinces and in all the variants between North and South India cooking.

Coriander seed is one of the principal ingredients of a curry mixture. Cocoanut is used a great deal in the southern half of India. It adds to the nutritive quality. When well made there is no dish with a more distinctive taste than a good curry. And the heat of it is a good thermostat, a sort of balancer between the Indian himself and the outer air which is cooler than he is by contrast.

CURRY POWDER

1 oz. coriander seed
1 tsp. caraway seed
1 tsp. black pepper
1 tsp. red pepper
6 tsp. turmeric
1 tsp. cloves
4 tsp. cinnamon
6 cardamon seeds

Grind in a small hand mill or coffee mill, sift three or four times together and dry thoroughly in the oven. Two teaspoons of this mixture is quantity sufficient to flavor a dish using a pound of meat as a base.

BEEF CURRY

2 pounds fresh beef (round)
1 large Bermuda onion
2 tbsp. butter or vegetable fat
1 rounded tbsp. curry powder
2 cups water
1 cup canned peas
1 large potato or 2 apples
salt, q.s.

Peel and slice onion and fry in the fat. Remove when light brown. Stir the curry powder in the fat and sear the meat, which has been cut in cubes, only until juices are sealed in. Salt to taste, return onion, and simmer in the water slowly until tender. A half hour before serving meal, add the potato diced raw or the apples (if apples are used, not as soon as potato) and then the peas. Use more water if necessary for plenty of gravy.

Serve with hot boiled rice.

CURRIED ONIONS

4 cups sliced onions
4 tbsp. butter
1 tsp. curry powder
2 tsp. lemon juice
1 tsp. salt
½ tsp. pepper

Sauté the onions in the butter until tender. Blend lemon juice and dry seasonings and stir in. Cook until onions begin to brown. Serve with steak.

DO PIYAZ

This is a curry and the name means *two-onion,* from the cooking method, i.e., part of the onion is fried and part ground.

1 lamb chop per person
6 small onions
3 tbsp. butter (In India it would be *ghee*)
¾ tsp. salt
½ tsp. curry powder
½ tsp. chili powder (optional)
2 tsp. ground onion (use onion salt)
⅛ tsp. garlic salt
½ cup water or stock

Peel and slice the onions and cook in hot butter. Remove from fat, combine all the condiments and add to butter. Brown the chops. Cover the chops with the cooked onion, add stock if necessary, and simmer until meat is tender and liquid is absorbed.

DHAL

Dhal is a legume of which there are many varieties. Commercially it looks like our dried split peas, somewhat, and the taste is similar. In North India yellow dhal is used more commonly. It is served with boiled rice, as a sauce or gravy. And it can be baked for a hearty luncheon dish or made into croquettes. The lentil is another similar legume.

       1 cup yellow *dhal*
   1½ tsp. salt
       2 red onions
       1 tsp. curry powder
       1 clove garlic (optional)
       3 tsbp. fat

Wash the *dhal*, soak until soft. Drain, add fresh water, and cook with 1 tsp. salt and 1 of the onions sliced, simmering until mushy. Meantime slice the other onion and cook in garlic-flavored fat. Add to the *dhal* mixture and cook slowly ten minutes more. Serve with hot rice.

IRELAND

TISSUE ONIONS

More to be dreamed of than eaten, for who is to get an Irish onion from the fields of Athenry? They grow the finest there and around Ballinasloe.

But one may cut a big sweet Bermuda into slices as thin as any onion's skin, and drown it off the knife in a bowl of Chablis. Season with pepper and salt so that you can see the pepper, chill in the refrigerator and serve with salad on a hot day, or with a cold joint of a winter Sunday night.

CONNAUGHT ONIONS

This is buttered onion pie, a glazed onion, parboiled and covered with a rich sauce of butter and caramel sugar, baked in a deep-dish pie.

ITALY

FRITTATA DI CIPOLLA

Onion Omelet from Italy.
       4 eggs
       6 tbsp. olive oil or butter
       1 large sweet onion

Break eggs into deep bowl; add salt and pepper to taste; beat lightly; slice onion wafer-thin. Heat half oil or butter in the skillet. Brown onion slightly for about 5 minutes. Remove; place in bowl. Add eggs; beat well. Heat balance of oil in skillet; cook eggs over low flame 3 to 5 minutes or until omelet is light and fluffy and browned on under side. Using spatula, turn over carefully. Brown lightly. Serves 4.

This recipe should have quotes around it, because I had it from a friend who is a native Sicilian.

JAPAN

SUKI YAKI

If only it could be that everyone might eat this first as I did, sailing home on a crack mail ship of a proud line. The Pacific was a very plain ocean but my ship had been named for a prince and there was an aura about the trip that made everything seem a little super. I had never been on the Pacific before. There were parties and pleasant people—a famous eastern baseball team sailed with us—and life was good. It was before there was any talk of war and all of us were friends.

Since then I have eaten *Suki Yaki* many times under less romantic circumstances, so I know that it is really good, and that the first time it wasn't just sea air and the novelty of watching my dinner cooked in a charcoal brazier set into the middle of the table.

The base of this is tender beef which your butcher will cut for you in almost paper thin strips, about an inch and a half wide.

    2 lbs. beef, cut thin
    2 tbsp. of melted beef suet
    2 onions
    2 scallions
    4 fresh mushrooms
      bamboo or bean sprouts
    2 stalks celery

2 tbsp. sugar
bean curd and soya sauce
salt, q.s.

Shred onions, scallions, celery, and mushrooms. Heat the skillet very hot and cook meat alone in the suet for a few minutes. Add the other ingredients, except the bean curd, sprinkling sugar and sauce on top. Cook, stirring occasionally, until the onion and scallions are tender. Add bean curd, blend contents again, and serve hot with rice.

Note: Chicken may be substituted for the beef.

RUSSIA

PILAV
(Lamb and Rice)

This is a good example of the way foods become identified with a particular country, yet are common to several. In India it is a *Pilao* and in Turkey and Armenia it becomes *Pilaff* and it is still lamb and rice.

2 lbs. lamb (chops are the best)
2 tbsp. fat
1 onion
2 carrots
1 cup stock
6 bay leaves
½ cup raisins
1 cup rice, washed and scalded
a few peppercorns
salt, q.s.

Brown the chops, then the onion and carrots, chopped, in the fat. Pour over stock and seasonings. Cook, covered, until meat is half done. Add rice and more stock if necessary. Cook until rice is tender and brown and all the stock is absorbed. Pile rice on a platter and chops on top. Bay leaves are left in for garnish.

SCOTLAND

COCK-A-LEEKIE SOUP

12 leeks
1 carrot
2 stalks celery
1 stewing chicken
2 quarts veal stock
   seasonings, q.s.

Clean and trim leeks and cut them in pieces about half an inch long. Sauté in butter with the carrot and celery, also cut small.

Clean the chicken as for roasting, but cook whole, in a large kettle with the veal stock and vegetables. It will take about 1½ hours or until bird is tender. Remove it to a platter and joint.

Lay the pieces in a serving tureen, and pour the thick soup over.

A very old recipe for this dish called for Jamaica pepper and suggested a few prunes be added half an hour before serving. There were those, then, who felt only an atheist could have so polluted it.

SOUTH AFRICA

BOBOTI
(Hash)

1 slice soft bread
1 cup milk
1 tbsp. butter
2 medium sized white onions
½ tsp. curry powder
1 tsp. salt
1 tbsp. sugar
2 tbsp. vinegar
2 cups of cold roast beef, chopped
2 eggs

Pour milk over the bread and soak. Peel and slice onions and sauté in the fat until soft, then add curry powder and salt.

Combine vinegar, sugar, and beef and add to first mixture.

Beat eggs lightly, pour over the bread and milk, and blend it with the meat and onions. Dot with bits of butter, in a shallow baking dish, and put in moderate oven for about a half hour or until set firm.

SPAIN

CHICKEN WITH MOLE SAUCE

This is a dish of Spanish extraction via the American Southwest. *Mole* is from *molecule,* meaning the fine blending of the sauce ingredients.

> 1 five-pound chicken
> ⅓ cup almonds
> 1 tbsp. peanuts
> 2 tsp. sesame seeds
> ½ tsp. cloves
> ⅓ stick cinnamon
> 4 chili peppers
> 1 cup fine bread crumbs
> 1 oz. bitter chocolate
> 1 Spanish onion
> 4 tbsp. butter, melted
> 1 tomato chopped
> 1 clove garlic, mashed

Have the chicken jointed Southern style. This is much easier to handle than the any-old-way-to-cut-it-apart method of a good many butchers. Clean the pieces thoroughly, removing all pin feathers, wash with hot and cold water and wipe with a damp cloth. Simmer in salted water until almost tender.

Meantime, grind and blend the nuts, seeds, spices, peppers, bread crumbs, chocolate and minced onion.

Remove the chicken from the broth, drain and brown in the melted butter. Add sauce ingredients to the broth and stir until well blended. Return the chicken to the broth, with the tomatoes and garlic and simmer uncovered until the meat is tender and the broth is thick.

Serve with rice.

SWEDEN

A SAUCE FOR HOT HAM

1½ cups stock in which ham has been boiled
1 small Spanish onion
1 carrot
8 whole allspice
6 cloves
1 bayleaf
1 cup pineapple juice
½ cup washed currants
1 tsp. prepared mustard
4 level tsp. flour
2 tbsp. brown sugar

Wash currants and soak, while chopping onion and carrot and cooking them in the ham stock, about 20 minutes.

Add pineapple juice, spices and bayleaf and cook 5 more minutes; add the currants and cook another five. Then remove the bayleaf.

Blend the mustard, flour, and sugar in a little water and add slowly to the hot liquid. Cook until thick.

Serve hot.

SWITZERLAND

SAUERBRATEN

Except for its dairy distinction, Swiss cooking is not uniquely Switzerland's. In the north the vigorous spicey foods of German ancestors predominate. In the south there is the influence of Italy in sauces and pastries, with a French taste expressed in seasonings and desserts in the west. But these very differences make for a unique blend that may be all Gaul at one meal or any of its three parts at another.

The north was to the fore in a Swiss household the day I first tasted *Sauerbraten*, but it will never be a German dish to me because Madame had made it herself and she came from the Lauterbrunnen Valley in the Bernese Alps, of the Swiss a Swiss, to the manner born, and how she could cook!

> 3–lb. pot roast of beef
> 2 cups cider vinegar
> 2 cups water
> 2 bay leaves
> 2 tsp. salt
> 1 tsp. peppercorns
> 4 tbsp. sugar
> 3 cloves
> 1 Spanish onion
> 1 garlic pod (optional)

Combine vinegar, water, and seasonings and heat through. Place the meat in a glass or earthenware bowl, deep enough for the liquid to cover and having a solid lid. Slice the onion over the meat and marinate it in the spiced vinegar for at least three days, turning it over every day.

When ready to cook, remove from the vinegar, and brown in hot fat, proceeding as for regular pot roast, using the vinegar liquid for any additional that is required. Carrots and onions may be cooked with it when partially done. Give the onions longer time than the carrots.

Serve with potato dumplings, which are traditional.

KARTOFFELKLOESSE

> 6 medium sized cold boiled poatoes
> 2 eggs
> 1½ tsp. salt
> ½ cup flour

Rice the potatoes; and add to a batter made of the remaining ingredients. Beat until fluffy. Make small balls about an inch through, coat with flour lightly and cook in kettle gravy.

SYRIA

ONIONS WITH RICE

1½ lbs. white onions
4 tbsp. olive oil
3 tbsp. lemon juice
1 clove
½ stick cinnamon
1 bay leaf
1 berry of allspice
½ can tomatoes (No. 2 can)
½ cup chicken broth

Slice and sauté the onions in the oil. Season with a little salt and cook slowly until a golden brown.

Sieve the tomatoes, combine with the broth and the seasonings, and add to the onions. Simmer until well blended. Take out bay leaf and serve with rice.

CHAPTER 11

Garlic

Allium Sativum

If Leekes you like
But do their smell dis-leeke
   Eat Onyuns
And you shall not smell the Leeke.

If you of Onyuns
Would the scent expelle
   Eat Garlicke,
And that shall drowne
   The Onyun's smelle.

ANON.

An old story is told of an older king, in Arabia, who was so pleased with the first onion that came his way that he gave the donor a fortune in gold and jewels. The traveler told the story of his luck to the next man he met. That man, it chanced, had a garlic bud which he had meant to plant. But if the king liked onions, how much more would he appreciate the potent garlic? And he dreamed a fine dream of the higher estate that would be his the next day. He would ask for a house instead of gold, and he would ask for a garden round the house instead of jewels. And in the garden he would plant much garlic to bring him even greater winnings. The whole kingdom would have garlic—for a price. But when the time came that the man was admitted to the king's antechamber, he had no opportunity to ask for anything. The king said, impatiently, "Ah, here you are at last. I understand you have something greater and finer than even my own most cherished possession. I will give it you gladly for the sake of that you have brought." And the garlic changed hands and the man was ushered out to be given—the king's onion!

Garlic grows in white bulbs made up of a number of segments called cloves, pink-skinned if the Italian variety and white if Mexican. They fit together in the paper-like case around them in almost the same way that Brazil nuts fit in theirs, or the sections do in an orange.

137

If one has a garden, even of pocket kerchief size, a few inches of space are enough for a bit of garlic. It can be grown from sets just as onions are, using one clove as a set, planted point up. That one will divide again and produce all the flavoring any family could want in a season, with some left over for the neighbors who grow flowers instead of vegetables.

Some die-hard gardeners, who have green fingers but no land, resort to flower pots to grow fresh kitchen seasonings. One clove of garlic in a common red clay flower pot should prove as useful and delightful as a clump of chives.

Try chopping a bit of fresh garlic top for flavoring the dishes which normally get the chives treatment; mashed potatoes for instance, and eggs and soup. BUT, always temper enthusiasm with caution. Be as canny as a Scot when you reach for the scissors or for a dry clove, whenever garlic appears in a recipe or on a list of flavor suggestions.

Old wives maintain that ghosts and vampires would never venture near garlic. Homer tells us that Nestor served garlic to his guest Machaon and Galen, a physician famous in old Rome in the first century, wrote of garlic as the countryman's best antidote and he prescribed it so. It has been found to have the same property for beasts as well, and one good meal of garlic completely purges a dog of worms. If allowed the run of a garden where it is growing, he will help himself and though of course he can't be borne in the house for some time after, it seems a question of choosing a lesser evil.

By Queen Elizabeth's time, the opprobrium garlic suffered after Galen had begun in England and the term *garlic-eater* meant a mean, low fellow. But that has not stopped the French from making a festival when the first garlic appears in the spring. And the popularity of our American salad bowl with its garlic concomitant, among adventurers in taste, is a full swing round the circle back to ancient Egypt again. To a real gourmet, gauging the degree of the garlic atom in the bowl is almost a religious rite.

William Shakespeare must have been either a good cook or a good trencherman and he could have been both, for his people talk so much about herbs and onions and garlic. But some modern cooks seem afraid to venture with garlic; others haven't time to do anything except open cans. A few more are in a culinary rut, though sometimes through no fault of their own. But when properly understood and used, garlic rewards the adventurous cook. Perhaps this chapter may change ruts into new roads, entice the timid and stay the hasty hand clutching a can opener.

TOSSED GREEN SALAD WITH GARLIC

One school of cooks holds that garlic shouldn't even touch the bowl in which the salad is tossed. Instead, they rub the clove on a dry crust of bread, a *chapon,* and allow it to wander in the green until serving time.

Another group has no part with bowl or bread. They mix the dry seasonings together, the sugar, salt, pepper, onion salt, paprika and sometimes mustard, to be moistened with the cut surface of a garlic clove. It is removed before the whole is combined with the greens and the vinegar and the oil.

Most all agree, however, that salad greens should be broken, not cut, into pieces for the bowl. Lettuce, iceberg or Boston, chicory, water cress, and romaine are all good, after they have been washed and completely chilled in the refrigerator to crisp them. Toss at the last minute possible before serving. And don't forget to remove the *chapon.*

Some people like to add cut tomatoes but unless they are drained well the juice is apt to dilute and spoil the tone of the vinegar, making the bouquet of flavors less piquant. Adding bits of whatever else is in the refrigerator, julienne ham or chicken, cooked baby limas, or peas, and hard-cooked egg, makes it a chef's salad, properly, and not strictly green, but if there is also some garlic in it . . .

A CHAPON FOR TOSSED SALAD

A *chapon* is the dry end or heel of a loaf of French bread. It is easy to grasp because of the round crusty shape. Rub this with a cut clove of garlic and toss with a green salad until ready to serve, when it is discarded. This method has an advantage over rubbing the salad bowl itself with the cut clove. If it is a wooden bowl there is the danger after repeated rubbings of making the salad bitter. The garlic grows old in the wood if the polish wears thin.

GARLIC CROUTONS

1 cup bread cubes
1 tbsp. cooking oil
1 clove garlic

Let the peeled garlic bud * stand in the oil for a few minutes. Remove it and toss in the bread cubes. Brown them, stirring frequently.

These may be used in a variety of ways: with creamed soup such as tomato or pea or chicken. Or, added at the last minute, they are welcome in some kinds of tossed salads. And what they can do to an otherwise plain omelet is worth trying to find out.

* Note: The garlic is not cut, to avoid the possibility of any particles remaining in the oil or frying too brown, thus making the croutons bitter. See page 145.

TOASTED GARLIC BREAD

1 long loaf of French bread
1 clove garlic
½ cup butter

The cook who likes to use garlic at all will find her own best way to serve French bread with garlic butter, gauging the degree of flavor by her family's taste. But all of us agree on one essential —cut the long loaf on the bias, not quite through the bottom crust, in inch-thick slashes.

Peel the clove and cut it or slice it and let it stand in the melted butter until the flavor permeates. It won't take long and you won't need much, whatever the family says. Remove.

Brush butter on with a pastry brush or spread with a knife on both sides of each slice. Push the loaf together again, wrap in its paper or use brown paper if it came without one, and set the whole in the oven, which should be only moderately hot, not more than 375°, for about 15 minutes. Before serving, snip the loaf apart with shears.

A super loaf can be made by sprinkling grated cheese on top after the garlic butter treatment and before setting in the oven, tying around with a string instead of the paper wrapper.

It's good either way, with or without paper or cheese.

GARLIC CASES FOR CREAMED MIXTURES.

Four large crusty Vienna rolls
2 tbsp. butter
½ clove garlic

Remove the tops of the rolls and hollow out. Put butter in a small saucepan over low heat and drop in the sliced garlic. Remove when the butter has melted and brush the insides of the rolls until all has been soaked in. Just before serving, run the rolls under the broiler flame to brown slightly before filling with the mixture of the evening or, it might be, for lunch.

The cases could also be made from a loaf of bread cut in four, an unsliced loaf of course; remove crusts, hollow the centers, butter and toast before filling.

One can dream up a dozen fillings that would happily follow soup, and precede a delicate fruit dessert, for a company luncheon. There might be fish in a rich cream sauce, or chicken livers in mushroom sauce, white meat of chicken alone in a golden à la king sauce, or creamed dried beef.

GARLIC BREAD IN SCALLOPED TOMATOES

Prepare a loaf as for toasted garlic bread but instead of following through the baking operation, cut the bread in cubes and use between the layers of the scallop, baking as usual. There could be also grated cheese on top.

ROAST LAMB WITH GARLIC

Quantity for four is not an item in this recipe, for one counts on using the part not eaten as the basis of other meals. And an eight pound roast, or as nearly that as possible before you get over into the mutton class, will have better flavor than a small one. If it is really a lamb roast that you want, look for the pale pink flesh and fine white fat which distinguish what the market knows as spring lamb from early summer to Christmas time.

When the meat is wiped free of butcher's block bits and you are ready to begin, start with a number of slits in the flesh in which you insert slivers of garlic clove, fresh parsley and if you want to go that far, bits of bacon. The amount of flavor depends again upon the family taste and your own judgment. If you omit the parsley and the bacon, go farther in the meat and make the slits for the garlic slivers right away down to the bone.

Then rub with the juice of one lemon (or substitute dry white wine) and follow with 1 tablespoon of olive oil. Salt and pepper too, of course, and when the roast is set on its rack in a shallow roasting pan, don't forget two cups of hot water for basting. Have a slow oven and allow 30-35 minutes per pound for the roasting.

For a leg of veal one can follow very nearly this same garlic routine. It is a mild meat and needs its flavor enhanced.

ZUCCHINI WITH GARLIC

These small green Italian squashes are becoming better known and garlic seems a natural flavor to add, considering their kindred home around the Mediterranean.

Two medium sized zucchini will be enough for four people if this is an auxiliary dish for dinner and not the main one.

Wash well. Cut off the ends but do not pare. Cut into thick slices and cook in a small amount of water (a half inch) with two teaspoons of salt in a covered kettle for about fifteen minutes, or until tender.

Drain and add a pinch of pepper and three tablespoons of butter and toss in one peeled clove of garlic. Cover again and let stand until the butter has melted. Remove the garlic, shake the kettle to be sure all the slices of zucchini are coated with the butter, and serve. Or, after the garlic is removed, the squash may be mashed and whipped with a little cream.

EGGS DELHI

6 eggs
4 large chicken livers (½ lb.)
3 tbsp. butter
⅓ cup light cream
1 clove garlic
1 tsp. salt
¼ tsp. curry powder

Melt butter and let garlic stand in it a few minutes, while livers are cut in small pieces. Sauté them in the garlic butter after removing the clove. Combine beaten eggs, cream and seasonings. Pour over livers and stir until soft and thick. Serve hot.

GARLIC-FLAVORED CHEESE
(as hors d'oeuvre)

Olives and garlic like each other. It's the blending, possibly. Try garlic salt in a little creamed cheese full of chopped bits of black olives. Crisp salted crackers are a good base. Don't spread beforehand, else the crackers will be clammy and unpleasant. Let the guests spread their own, or serve the mixture as a dip, with large potato chips.

GARLIC SALT

This may be bought already prepared but it loses strength after a few months. It is so easy to buy dry garlic, one clove at a time, that it is commendable to make one's own garlic salt freshly as it is required. It is worth trying certainly for this is the best known medium to control the degree of strength of this particular flavor. It is simply done. Peel a clove of garlic, cut it through and rub it into table salt until you have sufficient for the need of the moment. One clove is enough to flavor two heaping tablespoons of salt. If it is too much for your taste, then experiment will give you the answer to a pleasanter equation.

GARLIC VINEGAR

Prepared garlic vinegar is trustworthy unless it proves too strong for the family taste. In that case it can be made at home by using a good plain vinegar and adding a peeled clove. The strength then depends on you and how long you leave the clove in it.

DILL PICKLES WITH GARLIC

To a jar of commercially prepared dill pickles add one or two peeled cloves of garlic, according to the size of the jar and the taste of the family, and let stand for a week or two, until the flavor has thoroughly permeated the pickles.

If you have a garden, and dill and cucumbers in the garden, get out the glass jars and make your own. Prepare a brine from 1 quart of vinegar, 2 quarts water, and 1 cup cooking salt. Select the size of cucumber best suited for your needs and pack them into sterilized jars. For each jar provide the following:

> one large dill flower
> one clove garlic
> one dried chili pepper
> one slice white onion
> one peppercorn
> one clove

Cover with the hot brine and seal. Let stand one week before serving.

Slices of dill pickle, cut crosswise or on the bias, and well drained are a palatable addition to a tray of hors d'oeuvre.

GARLIC FLAVORING MISCELLANY

Rubbing a clove of garlic in the bowl need not be reserved for salads:

There is the morning toast, on which the fried or the scrambled egg will be served;

There is the platter for the cold sliced roast beef, the white meat of chicken, the roast turkey, and the Sunday night cold cuts. But rub with a light hand.

If you aren't serving garlic butter with a broiled steak, at least rub the platter with a cut clove before taking the meat to the table, where the carver waits but not willing to wait for more than a gesture on your part.

Crush a garlic clove in the oil or butter in which you plan to fry chops. Remove before cooking the meat.

A poultry item. Rub the flesh of a chicken just before rolling it in flour to fry, instead of frying it in garlic-flavored fat. Use garlic with chicken profusely only when following a recipe for Southern style or hot country methods.

Warning. This is like the sign "Low Bridge." When flavoring fat or butter with garlic never allow the slices or the half clove to brown completely. If it burns it smells like a chemistry experiment of the more loathsome sort, which everybody in class feels might better be buried.

To protect your fingers from the raw garlic odor, hold the clove with a fork. Or get one of the new little gadgets of post-war manufacture like a small mortar and pestle for breaking down a clove to cook with. With one of these it isn't necessary to touch the garlic after the skin is broken. To deodorize the fork or your fingers, soap and *cold* water are best.

The use of garlic in cooking is completely a question of a light hand and good judgment for it is the most vigorous individualist in the garden. Be cautious at first, careful always and, if in doubt, a mite near, as they say in New England. With experience, form and amounts and handling will become instinctive. Consider yourself a graduate when guests are obliged to guess before they identify the ingredient which makes them break down and ask for the recipe.

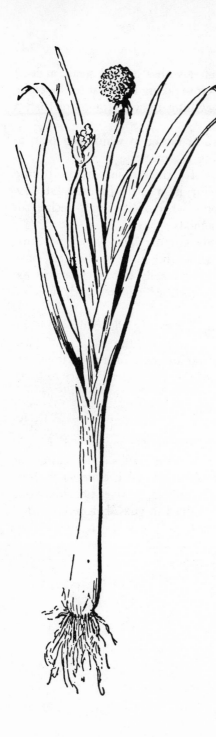

CHAPTER 12

Leeks

Allium Porrum

Leeks is goot
*Fluellen to Pistol
in Henry V.*

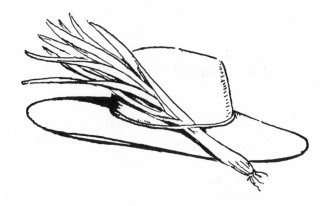

The leek is the aristocrat of the edible alliums, probably because it does not taint the breath. Neither is it eaten raw.

It enters this picture from obscurity in Siberia, and is traceable via Rome to the British Isles where the Welsh made it their own, peculiarly, in battle. Legend runs that back in the sixth century, when the Welsh were fighting the Saxons, King David ordered his soldiers to wear leeks in their bonnets for identification in the fighting. The long leaves waving about in the melee were as prominent as the plumes of a knight. So the vegetable became a national emblem for Wales, and Welshmen still turn out on St. David's Day, March twenty-second, with leeks in their hats, because an army once mustered for battle near a field of them.

To prepare leeks for cooking, cut off the shaggy beard of fine roots and remove leaves just above the point at which the outside ones begin. Rinse thoroughly under a spray tap to be sure no grit remains in the inner leaf pockets. Thick ones should be sliced lengthwise before boiling. They combine in the same way onions do with other vegetables, imparting a mild flavor.

The tops are also edible, cooked, and can be used in soup and vegetable recipes calling for leeks. This vegetable is much used in French cooking and is often termed *poor man's asparagus*. It can be served buttered or with hollandaise sauce. See the recipe for Armenian Leeks on page 119.

BOILED LEEKS

Wash well and boil or steam until tender. Serve with a cream sauce, garnished with crumbled hard-cooked egg yolk or buttered crumbs.

BRAISED LEEKS

3 bunches leeks
1 medium sized Bermuda onion
2 tbsp. butter
2 cups beef bouillon
2 whole cloves
1 bay leaf
½ tsp. salt
⅛ tsp. pepper

Cut off tops within 1½ inches of white part. Sauté onion in butter until lightly browned; add leeks, stock, and seasonings. Cover and simmer about 30 minutes, or until leeks are tender and stock has almost evaporated. Serve at once on hot platter.

HOT LEEK SOUP

4 thick leeks
4 medium sized potatoes
2 tbsp. butter
4 cups stock (chicken or veal)
yolk of one egg
2 cups coffee cream
⅛ tsp. nutmeg
salt and pepper, q.s.
1 tbsp. chopped chives (for top)

Wash leeks carefully and trim as for boiled leeks. Slice crosswise and sauté in butter. Slice potatoes thin, and cook together. Don't let the potatoes fry. Cover with the stock and cook, covered, until both are soft. Drain and sieve and combine with hot stock for purée.

Beat the egg yolk lightly and gradually combine with some of the stock, then add to the rest of the soup. Check seasonings here, and add more if stock has not been sufficiently salted in preparation. Add nutmeg. Pour in the cream and heat but do not boil. Garnish with chives and serve.

For a chilled cream of leek soup, see Vichysoisse on page 123.

LEEK SALAD

Boil stalks and drain with leaf end hung down until all moisture has dripped out. Marinate in a spicy French dressing and serve cold.

LEEKS VINAIGRETTE

Use the thinnings from the garden, like scallions, cook until tender and serve Vinaigrette (see page 84).

LEEKS AU GRATIN

> 12 leeks
> 1 cup Sauce Veloute
> ¼ lb. any good sharp cheese
> seasonings to taste

The bunches grow smaller as leeks grow larger. Slice thick ones lengthwise for even cooking. Cut in short lengths for this dish.

Drain the cooked leeks, arrange in a casserole, and pour over the Sauce Veloute, hot. Cover with thin slices of cheese or in grated form, run under the broiler until it melts and serve at once.

CHAPTER 13

Chives
Allium Schoenoprasum

Chives earn their way doubly as flower and food. The plump purple bloom-heads, somewhat clover-shaped, are ornament anywhere in the garden. And the spicy flavor of the freshly chopped hollow-tube leaves adds piquancy to many dishes in the kitchen.

To Grow Chives Growing from seed is the harder way but it can be done. The chief drawback is the time it takes—two years from germination to the table. This is all right if your only interest is an unusual border for a flower bed, or a difficult spot in a rock cranny. But for soup and salad it's a bit long to wait and a short-cut is to buy a clump at the grocer's in the spring and set out the tiny plants. They will provide juicy tops for snips in anything you fancy all summer and in the autumn from those that have not been allowed to flower a few can be potted for the kitchen window-sill, allowing the snipping sorties to continue. The small bulb is edible, but if left in the ground or pot it will produce new shoots of leaves.

Chives seem to have marched modestly through history, and to have achieved only cursory attention from Webster who says it is a "perennial plant allied to the onion." Cooks and chefs alike are grateful for the relationship and have made good use of it, for the story of chives in the kitchen is abundant.

BAKED EGGS

1 egg per person
1 strip of bacon for each egg
chive butter (see page 156)

Brush bottom and sides of the cups in a muffin cluster with chive butter. Cut the bacon strips in two, cook half done in a skillet and drain off grease. Place the halves crisscross in each muffin cup and break an egg in the center. Bake in a hot oven until the eggs are set. This can be done with halves of fresh tomato substituted for the eggs. But don't leave the chives out. Garnish with fresh parsley and serve with toast.

CHIVES WITH HARD-COOKED EGGS

As a variation to the eternal mustard with which we point up the mildness of eggs for stuffing or sandwich filling or hors d'oeuvre, try chives instead. They will go, hardily, wherever mustard does, and be as welcome.

CHIVES IN CREAMED EGGS

Hardcook one egg per person for a luncheon dish. Make ¼ cup for each of basic white sauce, seasoned with paprika. Add the sliced or quartered eggs and chopped chives, in a proportion of one teaspoon to four eggs. Cook until the seasonings and sauce and eggs are thoroughly blended, so that the dish will have a delicate yellow shade, a little lighter than the egg yolks. I am sure one egg per person will not be enough.

CHIVES IN SCRAMBLED EGGS

6 eggs (for four people)
⅓ cup milk
½ tbsp. chopped chives
2 tbsp. butter
salt and pepper, q.s.

Beat eggs and milk together with electric beater until very light. Fold in the chopped chives and seasoning by hand.

Melt the butter in a heavy iron skillet in time to pour in the beaten ingredients as soon as they are blended. Allow the mixture to form an edge in the hot butter, then tilt the pan and pull the firm portion back with your spatula. The remaining liquid can then run onto the greased surface in the same way. Repeat, until the eggs are firm but soft. If you are dexterous this mixture can be rolled in half in the skillet and tipped onto a hot platter as one does an omelet, but don't be discouraged if it breaks because it probably will.

It seems superfluous to add that the rest of the meal should be ready and waiting for the exact minute that the scramble operation is completed. But some cooks do forget to set the table first or to start the toaster while the eggs are first settling into the hot butter. You do it with that mythical other pair of hands that cooks are supposed to have.

DUMPLINGS WITH CHIVES

1 cup sifted all purpose flour
2 tsp. baking powder
½ tsp. salt
½ cup cold water or milk
1 tbsp. chopped chives
¼ tsp. nutmeg

Sift flour, baking powder, salt, and nutmeg. Add chives and moisten with the milk to make a soft dough.

The secret of good dumplings is to combine ingredients quickly and with as few motions as possible after the milk is added. This one is recommended for chicken or veal for the added flavor to these mild meats.

Drop by spoonfuls on the top of the simmering stew. If the dumpling dough is a little too moist and sticks to the spoon, try dipping the spoon in ice water before taking up the next dumpling. This amount should make about six. When all are formed, cover the kettle tightly and cook for about ten minutes, not uncovering in the meantime.

BAKING POWDER BISCUITS WITH CHIVES

    1 cup all purpose flour
    1 tsp. salt
    2 tsp. (rounded) baking powder
    3 tbsp. (rounded) shortening
    1 tbsp. chopped chives
    ⅓ to ½ cup milk

Sift flour once and measure one cup into sifter. Measure salt and baking powder and add to flour. Sift these dry ingredients together into a mixing bowl. Cut in shortening with a pastry blender until the mixture looks like coarse meal. Add chives.

Measure milk and use just enough to make a soft dough; any slight variation in the amount of flour governs the use of the full quantity of milk given. Cut with floured biscuit cutter after patting the dough into a circle about 1½ inches thick on a pastry board.

This makes 16 small biscuits.

Bake twelve minutes in a very hot oven.

CHIVES IN MAYONNAISE

    ⅔ of a cup of any good mayonnaise
    2 tbsp. chopped chives
    1 tbsp. minced parsley

Blend well and let stand for the flavor to permeate well. This is good for meat or fish salads. For the latter it may be thinned with a little lemon juice.

CHIVES IN OIL DRESSING

3 tbsp. oil (olive or salad)
1 tbsp. herb vinegar
1 tbsp. finely minced chives
1 tsp. sugar
1 tsp. salt
¼ tsp. paprika
⅛ tsp. black pepper
1 tsp. onion salt

Combine dry ingredients. Blend with the oil and vinegar in a glass jar. Toss in the chives last. Shake thoroughly until all are well blended, and shake again before pouring over a fresh vegetable salad. More can be made at one time by increasing each ingredient in proportion.

CHIVES IN MASHED POTATOES

Cook and mash, as is your custom. Whipped with seasonings and cream by hand or an electric beater, they should be fluffy and dry before going to the table.

I hope it is also your habit to serve them as they did when I used to visit a farm place as a child. The fluffy potatoes were put in a large tureen. A hollow was made in the middle of the mound with the back of a big spoon. A large lump of butter was allowed to melt there, like a little yellow lake. Then they dusted the whole top with black pepper.

The only reason chives were not added, I am sure, is that they were not the fashion then. But they are now, so add another dusting, after the pepper, of finely minced chives. The first spoonful of potato served will push the rest deep down in and the flavor will go all through and there won't be a dime's worth left to make potato cakes for lunch tomorrow.

CHIVE BUTTER

Cream butter and add half as much finely chopped chives in a two-tablespoons-of-butter to one-of-chives proportion. Force through a fine sieve. The flavor range for its use is as wide as your imagination. Mine says seven at the moment.

1. On top of baked potato, which has been slit and pushed open ready for the butter and the paprika and the *whatever* routine.

2. Optional spread for bread at a make-your-own sandwich party.

3. On a mound of rice waiting for its topping of creamed chicken.

4. To butter hot carrots, or lima beans that are a little older than babies.

5. With frenched stringed beans, drained and hot and ready for the trimmings.

6. A little paper case full, melted and still hot, to go with an artichoke for dip.

7. With lemon for hot broiled fish.

CHIVES AND CHEESE

Chives are an ideal addition to the bland base in cottage cheese or cream cheese for many combinations with bread and fruit and vegetables in the familiar salad and sandwich.

Blend one container of light cream with one of cream cottage cheese. Add seasonings, such as salt, pepper, onion salt, chopped chives, minced parsley, finely cut green pepper, and let stand in the refrigerator until the flavors have worked all through the cheese.

This can be eaten as a main dish for luncheon, with bread and butter. It will make a new and attractive dip for potato chip scoops on an hors d'oeuvre tray. It will make a good spread for rye or whole wheat sandwiches, little round ones with open faces centered with half a walnut, half of a big pecan, or a slice of stuffed olive and the edge dusted with paprika, just a little for color's sake, rather than flavor at that spot.

CHIVES AS DECOR

Many foods are pale and unattractive, even when possessing superb flavor; the eye needs help then to guide the hand to spoon or fork. A layered sandwich, iced with smooth cream cheese can be garnished with fine particles of chopped chives on top and be the better therefor.

Then there are the soups which need an artist's hand, on the same principle as touching up a photograph. Paprika and chopped chives on potato soup give it distinction. That is why Vichysoisse is never served without its green. A chef wouldn't, anyway.

Other uses will occur to the cook who likes to cut her own way through the jungle. One thing always leads to another. It is a good leading if you don't decorate to the point of disguise. That's another subject, however. And chives will let you know if you overdo them.

CHAPTER 14

By-Product

Notable as a conclusion to this brief for the versatility of the onion family are the many ways in which they have become associated since ancient times with the traditions, history, social customs, religion, and superstitions of people.

Two rivers bear the name, Onion River in Vermont, and L'Oignon in Burgundy, for no more apparent reason than that wild ones grew on their banks.

The onion has given pattern and distinction to ceramics. The possession of a set of Delft ware in the famous design of Meissen manufacture was a criterion of the owner's social position in the old days in Germany. American women are now haunting antique shops, turning up treasure here and there to assemble blue onions in sets again, their only criterion something useful and beautiful.

Architects have found inspiration in the form and smooth symmetry of the lily bulb's rounded sides, as witness the five onion-shaped domes on the Cathedral of the Assumption in Moscow, which was the coronation church under the Tsarist regime. There are other churches in Europe with onion domes and the term seems an accepted classification in the art world.

The association of onions with religion which had its symbolic beginnings in ancient Egypt still prevails. Hindu priests in South India are forbidden ever to eat them, nor may widows indulge their craving. Only those who know Indian food and the part onions play in curries can fully appreciate such a law. A ban exists on onions for four months of the year to the rest of the devout there, which is probably traceable to some long-forgotten tabu. It is recalled that the priests in Egypt tried to persuade their people not to touch onions or garlic.

In Brazil gardeners seriously believe that onions will not grow if they are not planted on Good Friday. In Orange County, New York, which is a famous onion-growing region, they have a ceremony called the Blessing of the Seeds, at planting time. And there is the English superstition that one must buy onions only in a shop that has two doors.

In its own realm, food, the onion has given fame to the chefs, Bechamel, Soubise and Savarin, who have raised it from social ostracism to an honored place on their menus and in their sauces, so that onionophiles no longer need hide their secret passion.

And finally, the ONION has given me something to talk about with great joy and no tears at all.

Index

A CATALOGUE OF SELECTED DOVER BOOKS
IN ALL FIELDS OF INTEREST

A CATALOGUE OF SELECTED DOVER BOOKS
IN ALL FIELDS OF INTEREST

LEATHER TOOLING AND CARVING, Chris H. Groneman. One of few books concentrating on tooling and carving, with complete instructions and grid designs for 39 projects ranging from bookmarks to bags. 148 illustrations. 111pp. 7⅞ x 10.
23061-9 Pa. $2.50

THE CODEX NUTTALL, A PICTURE MANUSCRIPT FROM ANCIENT MEXICO, as first edited by Zelia Nuttall. Only inexpensive edition, in full color, of a pre-Columbian Mexican (Mixtec) book. 88 color plates show kings, gods, heroes, temples, sacrifices. New explanatory, historical introduction by Arthur G. Miller. 96pp. 11⅜ x 8½.
23168-2 Pa. $7.50

AMERICAN PRIMITIVE PAINTING, Jean Lipman. Classic collection of an enduring American tradition. 109 plates, 8 in full color—portraits, landscapes, Biblical and historical scenes, etc., showing family groups, farm life, and so on. 80pp. of lucid text. 8⅜ x 11¼.
22815-0 Pa. $5.00

WILL BRADLEY: HIS GRAPHIC ART, edited by Clarence P. Hornung. Striking collection of work by foremost practitioner of Art Nouveau in America: posters, cover designs, sample pages, advertisements, other illustrations. 97 plates, including 8 in full color and 19 in two colors. 97pp. 9⅜ x 12¼.
20701-3 Pa. $4.00
22120-2 Clothbd. $10.00

AN ATLAS OF ANATOMY FOR ARTISTS, Fritz Schider. Finest text, working book. Full text, plus anatomical illustrations; plates by great artists showing anatomy. 593 illustrations. 192pp. 7⅞ x 10¾.
20241-0 Clothbd. $6.95

THE GIBSON GIRL AND HER AMERICA, Charles Dana Gibson. 155 finest drawings of effervescent world of 1900-1910: the Gibson Girl and her loves, amusements, adventures, Mr. Pipp, etc. Selected by E. Gillon; introduction by Henry Pitz. 144pp. 8¼ x 11⅜.
21986-0 Pa. $3.50

STAINED GLASS CRAFT, J.A.F. Divine, G. Blachford. One of the very few books that tell the beginner exactly what he needs to know: planning cuts, making shapes, avoiding design weaknesses, fitting glass, etc. 93 illustrations. 115pp.
22812-6 Pa. $1.75

AUSTRIAN COOKING AND BAKING, Gretel Beer. Authentic thick soups, wiener schnitzel, veal goulash, more, plus dumplings, puff pastries, nut cakes, sacher tortes, other great Austrian desserts. 224pp. USO 23220-4 Pa. $2.50

CHEESES OF THE WORLD, U.S.D.A. Dictionary of cheeses containing descriptions of over 400 varieties of cheese from common Cheddar to exotic Surati. Up to two pages are given to important cheeses like Camembert, Cottage, Edam, etc. 151pp. 22831-2 Pa. $1.50

TRITTON'S GUIDE TO BETTER WINE AND BEER MAKING FOR BEGINNERS, S.M. Tritton. All you need to know to make family-sized quantities of over 100 types of grape, fruit, herb, vegetable wines; plus beers, mead, cider, more. 11 illustrations. 157pp. USO 22528-3 Pa. $2.25

DECORATIVE LABELS FOR HOME CANNING, PRESERVING, AND OTHER HOUSEHOLD AND GIFT USES, Theodore Menten. 128 gummed, perforated labels, beautifully printed in 2 colors. 12 versions in traditional, Art Nouveau, Art Deco styles. Adhere to metal, glass, wood, most plastics. 24pp. 8¼ x 11. 23219-0 Pa. $2.00

FIVE ACRES AND INDEPENDENCE, Maurice G. Kains. Great back-to-the-land classic explains basics of self-sufficient farming: economics, plants, crops, animals, orchards, soils, land selection, host of other necessary things. Do not confuse with skimpy faddist literature; Kains was one of America's greatest agriculturalists. 95 illustrations. 397pp. 20974-1 Pa. $3.00

GROWING VEGETABLES IN THE HOME GARDEN, U.S. Dept. of Agriculture. Basic information on site, soil conditions, selection of vegetables, planting, cultivation, gathering. Up-to-date, concise, authoritative. Covers 60 vegetables. 30 illustrations. 123pp. 23167-4 Pa. $1.35

FRUITS FOR THE HOME GARDEN, Dr. U.P. Hedrick. A chapter covering each type of garden fruit, advice on plant care, soils, grafting, pruning, sprays, transplanting, and much more! Very full. 53 illustrations. 175pp. 22944-0 Pa. $2.50

GARDENING ON SANDY SOIL IN NORTH TEMPERATE AREAS, Christine Kelway. Is your soil too light, too sandy? Improve your soil, select plants that survive under such conditions. Both vegetables and flowers. 42 photos. 148pp. USO 23199-2 Pa. $2.50

THE FRAGRANT GARDEN: A BOOK ABOUT SWEET SCENTED FLOWERS AND LEAVES, Louise Beebe Wilder. Fullest, best book on growing plants for their fragrances. Descriptions of hundreds of plants, both well-known and overlooked. 407pp. 23071-6 Pa. **$4.00**

EASY GARDENING WITH DROUGHT-RESISTANT PLANTS, Arno and Irene Nehrling. Authoritative guide to gardening with plants that require a minimum of water: seashore, desert, and rock gardens; house plants; annuals and perennials; much more. 190 illustrations. 320pp. 23230-1 Pa. $3.50

DECORATIVE ALPHABETS AND INITIALS, edited by Alexander Nesbitt. 91 complete alphabets (medieval to modern), 3924 decorative initials, including Victorian novelty and Art Nouveau. 192pp. 7¾ x 10¾.   20544-4 Pa. $4.00

CALLIGRAPHY, Arthur Baker. Over 100 original alphabets from the hand of our greatest living calligrapher: simple, bold, fine-line, richly ornamented, etc. —all strikingly original and different, a fusion of many influences and styles. 155pp. 11⅜ x 8¼.   22895-9 Pa. $4.50

MONOGRAMS AND ALPHABETIC DEVICES, edited by Hayward and Blanche Cirker. Over 2500 combinations, names, crests in very varied styles: script engraving, ornate Victorian, simple Roman, and many others. 226pp. 8⅛ x 11.
22330-2 Pa. $5.00

THE BOOK OF SIGNS, Rudolf Koch. Famed German type designer renders 493 symbols: religious, alchemical, imperial, runes, property marks, etc. Timeless. 104pp. 6⅛ x 9¼.   20162-7 Pa. $1.75

200 DECORATIVE TITLE PAGES, edited by Alexander Nesbitt. 1478 to late 1920's. Baskerville, Dürer, Beardsley, W. Morris, Pyle, many others in most varied techniques. For posters, programs, other uses. 222pp. 8⅜ x 11¼.   21264-5 Pa. $5.00

DICTIONARY OF AMERICAN PORTRAITS, edited by Hayward and Blanche Cirker. 4000 important Americans, earliest times to 1905, mostly in clear line. Politicians, writers, soldiers, scientists, inventors, industrialists, Indians, Blacks, women, outlaws, etc. Identificatory information. 756pp. 9¼ x 12¾. 21823-6 Clothbd. $30.00

ART FORMS IN NATURE, Ernst Haeckel. Multitude of strangely beautiful natural forms: Radiolaria, Foraminifera, jellyfishes, fungi, turtles, bats, etc. All 100 plates of the 19th century evolutionist's Kunstformen der Natur (1904). 100pp. 9⅜ x 12¼.   22987-4 Pa. $4.00

DECOUPAGE: THE BIG PICTURE SOURCEBOOK, Eleanor Rawlings. Make hundreds of beautiful objects, over 550 florals, animals, letters, shells, period costumes, frames, etc. selected by foremost practitioner. Printed on one side of page. 8 color plates. Instructions. 176pp. 9³⁄₁₆ x 12¼.   23182-8 Pa. $5.00

AMERICAN FOLK DECORATION, Jean Lipman, Eve Meulendyke. Thorough coverage of all aspects of wood, tin, leather, paper, cloth decoration — scapes, humans, trees, flowers, geometrics — and how to make them. Full instructions. 233 illustrations, 5 in color. 163pp. 8⅜ x 11¼.   22217-9 Pa. $3.95

WHITTLING AND WOODCARVING, E.J. Tangerman. Best book on market; clear, full. If you can cut a potato, you can carve toys, puzzles, chains, caricatures, masks, patterns, frames, decorate surfaces, etc. Also covers serious wood sculpture. Over 200 photos. 293pp.   20965-2 Pa. $3.00

MODERN CHESS STRATEGY, Ludek Pachman. The use of the queen, the active king, exchanges, pawn play, the center, weak squares, etc. Section on rook alone worth price of the book. Stress on the moderns. Often considered the most important book on strategy. 314pp. 20290-9 Pa. $3.50

CHESS STRATEGY, Edward Lasker. One of half-dozen great theoretical works in chess, shows principles of action above and beyond moves. Acclaimed by Capablanca, Keres, etc. 282pp. USO 20528-2 Pa. $3.00

CHESS PRAXIS, THE PRAXIS OF MY SYSTEM, Aron Nimzovich. Founder of hypermodern chess explains his profound, influential theories that have dominated much of 20th century chess. 109 illustrative games. 369pp. 20296-8 Pa. $3.50

HOW TO PLAY THE CHESS OPENINGS, Eugene Znosko-Borovsky. Clear, profound examinations of just what each opening is intended to do and how opponent can counter. Many sample games, questions and answers. 147pp. 22795-2 Pa. $2.00

THE ART OF CHESS COMBINATION, Eugene Znosko-Borovsky. Modern explanation of principles, varieties, techniques and ideas behind them, illustrated with many examples from great players. 212pp. 20583-5 Pa. $2.50

COMBINATIONS: THE HEART OF CHESS, Irving Chernev. Step-by-step explanation of intricacies of combinative play. 356 combinations by Tarrasch, Botvinnik, Keres, Steinitz, Anderssen, Morphy, Marshall, Capablanca, others, all annotated. 245 pp. 21744-2 Pa. $3.00

HOW TO PLAY CHESS ENDINGS, Eugene Znosko-Borovsky. Thorough instruction manual by fine teacher analyzes each piece individually; many common endgame situations. Examines games by Steinitz, Alekhine, Lasker, others. Emphasis on understanding. 288pp. 21170-3 Pa. $2.75

MORPHY'S GAMES OF CHESS, Philip W. Sergeant. Romantic history, 54 games of greatest player of all time against Anderssen, Bird, Paulsen, Harrwitz; 52 games at odds; 52 blindfold; 100 consultation, informal, other games. Analyses by Anderssen, Steinitz, Morphy himself. 352pp. 20386-7 Pa. $4.00

500 MASTER GAMES OF CHESS, S. Tartakower, J. du Mont. Vast collection of great chess games from 1798-1938, with much material nowhere else readily available. Fully annotated, arranged by opening for easier study. 665pp. 23208-5 Pa. $6.00

THE SOVIET SCHOOL OF CHESS, Alexander Kotov and M. Yudovich. Authoritative work on modern Russian chess. History, conceptual background. 128 fully annotated games (most unavailable elsewhere) by Botvinnik, Keres, Smyslov, Tal, Petrosian, Spassky, more. 390pp. 20026-4 Pa. $3.95

WONDERS AND CURIOSITIES OF CHESS, Irving Chernev. A lifetime's accumulation of such wonders and curiosities as the longest won game, shortest game, chess problem with mate in 1220 moves, and much more unusual material —356 items in all, over 160 complete games. 146 diagrams. 203pp. 23007-4 Pa. $3.50

SLEEPING BEAUTY, illustrated by Arthur Rackham. Perhaps the fullest, most delightful version ever, told by C.S. Evans. Rackham's best work. 49 illustrations. 110pp. 7⅞ x 10¾.
22756-1 Pa. $2.00

THE WONDERFUL WIZARD OF OZ, L. Frank Baum. Facsimile in full color of America's finest children's classic. Introduction by Martin Gardner. 143 illustrations by W.W. Denslow. 267pp.
20691-2 Pa. $3.00

GOOPS AND HOW TO BE THEM, Gelett Burgess. Classic tongue-in-cheek masquerading as etiquette book. 87 verses, 170 cartoons as Goops demonstrate virtues of table manners, neatness, courtesy, more. 88pp. 6½ x 9¼.
22233-0 Pa. $2.00

THE BROWNIES, THEIR BOOK, Palmer Cox. Small as mice, cunning as foxes, exuberant, mischievous, Brownies go to zoo, toy shop, seashore, circus, more. 24 verse adventures. 266 illustrations. 144pp. 6⅝ x 9¼.
21265-3 Pa. $2.50

BILLY WHISKERS: THE AUTOBIOGRAPHY OF A GOAT, Frances Trego Montgomery. Escapades of that rambunctious goat. Favorite from turn of the century America. 24 illustrations. 259pp.
22345-0 Pa. $2.75

THE ROCKET BOOK, Peter Newell. Fritz, janitor's kid, sets off rocket in basement of apartment house; an ingenious hole punched through every page traces course of rocket. 22 duotone drawings, verses. 48pp. 6⅞ x 8⅜.
22044-3 Pa. $1.50

PECK'S BAD BOY AND HIS PA, George W. Peck. Complete double-volume of great American childhood classic. Hennery's ingenious pranks against outraged pomposity of pa and the grocery man. 97 illustrations. Introduction by E.F. Bleiler. 347pp.
20497-9 Pa. $2.50

THE TALE OF PETER RABBIT, Beatrix Potter. The inimitable Peter's terrifying adventure in Mr. McGregor's garden, with all 27 wonderful, full-color Potter illustrations. 55pp. 4¼ x 5½.
USO 22827-4 Pa. $1.00

THE TALE OF MRS. TIGGY-WINKLE, Beatrix Potter. Your child will love this story about a very special hedgehog and all 27 wonderful, full-color Potter illustrations. 57pp. 4¼ x 5½.
USO 20546-0 Pa. $1.00

THE TALE OF BENJAMIN BUNNY, Beatrix Potter. Peter Rabbit's cousin coaxes him back into Mr. McGregor's garden for a whole new set of adventures. A favorite with children. All 27 full-color illustrations. 59pp. 4¼ x 5½.
USO 21102-9 Pa. $1.00

THE MERRY ADVENTURES OF ROBIN HOOD, Howard Pyle. Facsimile of original (1883) edition, finest modern version of English outlaw's adventures. 23 illustrations by Pyle. 296pp. 6½ x 9¼.
22043-5 Pa. $4.00

TWO LITTLE SAVAGES, Ernest Thompson Seton. Adventures of two boys who lived as Indians; explaining Indian ways, woodlore, pioneer methods. 293 illustrations. 286pp.
20985-7 Pa. $3.00

MANUAL OF THE TREES OF NORTH AMERICA, Charles S. Sargent. The basic survey of every native tree and tree-like shrub, 717 species in all. Extremely full descriptions, information on habitat, growth, locales, economics, etc. Necessary to every serious tree lover. Over 100 finding keys. 783 illustrations. Total of 986pp.
20277-1, 20278-X Pa., Two vol. set $9.00

BIRDS OF THE NEW YORK AREA, John Bull. Indispensable guide to more than 400 species within a hundred-mile radius of Manhattan. Information on range, status, breeding, migration, distribution trends, etc. Foreword by Roger Tory Peterson. 17 drawings; maps. 540pp.
23222-0 Pa. $6.00

THE SEA-BEACH AT EBB-TIDE, Augusta Foote Arnold. Identify hundreds of marine plants and animals: algae, seaweeds, squids, crabs, corals, etc. Descriptions cover food, life cycle, size, shape, habitat. Over 600 drawings. 490pp.
21949-6 Pa. $5.00

THE MOTH BOOK, William J. Holland. Identify more than 2,000 moths of North America. General information, precise species descriptions. 623 illustrations plus 48 color plates show almost all species, full size. 1968 edition. Still the basic book. Total of 551pp. 6½ x 9¼.
21948-8 Pa. $6.00

AN INTRODUCTION TO THE REPTILES AND AMPHIBIANS OF THE UNITED STATES, Percy A. Morris. All lizards, crocodiles, turtles, snakes, toads, frogs; life history, identification, habits, suitability as pets, etc. Non-technical, but sound and broad. 130 photos. 253pp.
22982-3 Pa. $3.00

OLD NEW YORK IN EARLY PHOTOGRAPHS, edited by Mary Black. Your only chance to see New York City as it was 1853-1906, through 196 wonderful photographs from N.Y. Historical Society. Great Blizzard, Lincoln's funeral procession, great buildings. 228pp. 9 x 12.
22907-6 Pa. $6.00

THE AMERICAN REVOLUTION, A PICTURE SOURCEBOOK, John Grafton. Wonderful Bicentennial picture source, with 411 illustrations (contemporary and 19th century) showing battles, personalities, maps, events, flags, posters, soldier's life, ships, etc. all captioned and explained. A wonderful browsing book, supplement to other historical reading. 160pp. 9 x 12.
23226-3 Pa. $4.00

PERSONAL NARRATIVE OF A PILGRIMAGE TO AL-MADINAH AND MECCAH, Richard Burton. Great travel classic by remarkably colorful personality. Burton, disguised as a Moroccan, visited sacred shrines of Islam, narrowly escaping death. Wonderful observations of Islamic life, customs, personalities. 47 illustrations. Total of 959pp.
21217-3, 21218-1 Pa., Two vol. set $10.00

INCIDENTS OF TRAVEL IN CENTRAL AMERICA, CHIAPAS, AND YUCATAN, John L. Stephens. Almost single-handed discovery of Maya culture; exploration of ruined cities, monuments, temples; customs of Indians. 115 drawings. 892pp.
22404-X, 22405-8 Pa., Two vol. set $8.00

JEWISH GREETING CARDS, Ed Sibbett, Jr. 16 cards to cut and color. Three say "Happy Chanukah," one "Happy New Year," others have no message, show stars of David, Torahs, wine cups, other traditional themes. 16 envelopes. 8¼ x 11.
23225-5 Pa. $2.00

AUBREY BEARDSLEY GREETING CARD BOOK, Aubrey Beardsley. Edited by Theodore Menten. 16 elegant yet inexpensive greeting cards let you combine your own sentiments with subtle Art Nouveau lines. 16 different Aubrey Beardsley designs that you can color or not, as you wish. 16 envelopes. 64pp. 8¼ x 11.
23173-9 Pa. $2.00

RECREATIONS IN THE THEORY OF NUMBERS, Albert Beiler. Number theory, an inexhaustible source of puzzles, recreations, for beginners and advanced. Divisors, perfect numbers. scales of notation, etc. 349pp.
21096-0 Pa. $4.00

AMUSEMENTS IN MATHEMATICS, Henry E. Dudeney. One of largest puzzle collections, based on algebra, arithmetic, permutations, probability, plane figure dissection, properties of numbers, by one of world's foremost puzzlists. Solutions. 450 illustrations. 258pp.
20473-1 Pa. $3.00

MATHEMATICS, MAGIC AND MYSTERY, Martin Gardner. Puzzle editor for Scientific American explains math behind: card tricks, stage mind reading, coin and match tricks, counting out games, geometric dissections. Probability, sets, theory of numbers, clearly explained. Plus more than 400 tricks, guaranteed to work. 135 illustrations. 176pp.
20335-2 Pa. $2.00

BEST MATHEMATICAL PUZZLES OF SAM LOYD, edited by Martin Gardner. Bizarre, original, whimsical puzzles by America's greatest puzzler. From fabulously rare Cyclopedia, including famous 14-15 puzzles, the Horse of a Different Color, 115 more. Elementary math. 150 illustrations. 167pp.
20498-7 Pa. $2.50

MATHEMATICAL PUZZLES FOR BEGINNERS AND ENTHUSIASTS, Geoffrey Mott-Smith. 189 puzzles from easy to difficult involving arithmetic, logic, algebra, properties of digits, probability. Explanation of math behind puzzles. 135 illustrations. 248pp.
20198-8 Pa. $2.75

BIG BOOK OF MAZES AND LABYRINTHS, Walter Shepherd. Classical, solid, and ripple mazes; short path and avoidance labyrinths; more — 50 mazes and labyrinths in all. 12 other figures. Full solutions. 112pp. 8⅛ x 11.
22951-3 Pa. $2.00

COIN GAMES AND PUZZLES, Maxey Brooke. 60 puzzles, games and stunts — from Japan, Korea, Africa and the ancient world, by Dudeney and the other great puzzlers, as well as Maxey Brooke's own creations. Full solutions. 67 illustrations. 94pp.
22893-2 Pa. $1.50

HAND SHADOWS TO BE THROWN UPON THE WALL, Henry Bursill. Wonderful Victorian novelty tells how to make flying birds, dog, goose, deer, and 14 others. 32pp. 6½ x 9¼.
21779-5 Pa. $1.25

THE JOURNAL OF HENRY D. THOREAU, edited by Bradford Torrey, F.H. Allen. Complete reprinting of 14 volumes, 1837-1861, over two million words; the source-books for Walden, etc. Definitive. All original sketches, plus 75 photographs. Introduction by Walter Harding. Total of 1804pp. 8½ x 12¼.
20312-3, 20313-1 Clothbd., Two vol. set $50.00

MASTERS OF THE DRAMA, John Gassner. Most comprehensive history of the drama, every tradition from Greeks to modern Europe and America, including Orient. Covers 800 dramatists, 2000 plays; biography, plot summaries, criticism, theatre history, etc. 77 illustrations. 890pp. 20100-7 Clothbd. $10.00

GHOST AND HORROR STORIES OF AMBROSE BIERCE, Ambrose Bierce. 23 modern horror stories: The Eyes of the Panther, The Damned Thing, etc., plus the dream-essay Visions of the Night. Edited by E.F. Bleiler. 199pp. 20767-6 Pa. $2.00

BEST GHOST STORIES, Algernon Blackwood. 13 great stories by foremost British 20th century supernaturalist. The Willows, The Wendigo, Ancient Sorceries, others. Edited by E.F. Bleiler. 366pp. USO 22977-7 Pa. $3.00

THE BEST TALES OF HOFFMANN, E.T.A. Hoffmann. 10 of Hoffmann's most important stories, in modern re-editings of standard translations: Nutcracker and the King of Mice, The Golden Flowerpot, etc. 7 illustrations by Hoffmann. Edited by E.F. Bleiler. 458pp. 21793-0 Pa. $3.95

BEST GHOST STORIES OF J.S. LEFANU, J. Sheridan LeFanu. 16 stories by greatest Victorian master: Green Tea, Carmilla, Haunted Baronet, The Familiar, etc. Mostly unavailable elsewhere. Edited by E.F. Bleiler. 8 illustrations. 467pp.
20415-4 Pa. $4.00

SUPERNATURAL HORROR IN LITERATURE, H.P. Lovecraft. Great modern American supernaturalist brilliantly surveys history of genre to 1930's, summarizing, evaluating scores of books. Necessary for every student, lover of form. Introduction by E.F. Bleiler. 111pp. 20105-8 Pa. $1.50

THREE GOTHIC NOVELS, ed. by E.F. Bleiler. Full texts Castle of Otranto, Walpole; Vathek, Beckford; The Vampyre, Polidori; Fragment of a Novel, Lord Byron. 331pp. 21232-7 Pa. $3.00

SEVEN SCIENCE FICTION NOVELS, H.G. Wells. Full novels. First Men in the Moon, Island of Dr. Moreau, War of the Worlds, Food of the Gods, Invisible Man, Time Machine, In the Days of the Comet. A basic science-fiction library. 1015pp.
USO 20264-X Clothbd. $6.00

LADY AUDLEY'S SECRET, Mary E. Braddon. Great Victorian mystery classic, beautifully plotted, suspenseful; praised by Thackeray, Boucher, Starrett, others. What happened to beautiful, vicious Lady Audley's husband? Introduction by Norman Donaldson. 286pp. 23011-2 Pa. $3.00

150 MASTERPIECES OF DRAWING, edited by Anthony Toney. 150 plates, early 15th century to end of 18th century; Rembrandt, Michelangelo, Dürer, Fragonard, Watteau, Wouwerman, many others. 150pp. 8⅜ x 11¼.   21032-4 Pa. $4.00

THE GOLDEN AGE OF THE POSTER, Hayward and Blanche Cirker. 70 extraordinary posters in full colors, from Maîtres de l'Affiche, Mucha, Lautrec, Bradley, Cheret, Beardsley, many others. 9⅜ x 12¼.   22753-7 Pa. $4.95
21718-3 Clothbd. $7.95

SIMPLICISSIMUS, selection, translations and text by Stanley Appelbaum. 180 satirical drawings, 16 in full color, from the famous German weekly magazine in the years 1896 to 1926. 24 artists included: Grosz, Kley, Pascin, Kubin, Kollwitz, plus Heine, Thöny, Bruno Paul, others. 172pp. 8½ x 12¼.   23098-8 Pa. $5.00
23099-6 Clothbd. $10.00

THE EARLY WORK OF AUBREY BEARDSLEY, Aubrey Beardsley. 157 plates, 2 in color: Manon Lescaut, Madame Bovary, Morte d'Arthur, Salome, other. Introduction by H. Marillier. 175pp. 8½ x 11.   21816-3 Pa. $4.00

THE LATER WORK OF AUBREY BEARDSLEY, Aubrey Beardsley. Exotic masterpieces of full maturity: Venus and Tannhäuser, Lysistrata, Rape of the Lock, Volpone, Savoy material, etc. 174 plates, 2 in color. 176pp. 8½ x 11. 21817-1 Pa. $4.00

DRAWINGS OF WILLIAM BLAKE, William Blake. 92 plates from Book of Job, Divine Comedy, Paradise Lost, visionary heads, mythological figures, Laocoön, etc. Selection, introduction, commentary by Sir Geoffrey Keynes. 178pp. 8½ x 11.   22303-5 Pa. $3.50

LONDON: A PILGRIMAGE, Gustave Doré, Blanchard Jerrold. Squalor, riches, misery, beauty of mid-Victorian metropolis; 55 wonderful plates, 125 other illustrations, full social, cultural text by Jerrold. 191pp. of text. 8⅛ x 11.
22306-X Pa. $5.00

THE COMPLETE WOODCUTS OF ALBRECHT DÜRER, edited by Dr. W. Kurth. 346 in all: Old Testament, St. Jerome, Passion, Life of Virgin, Apocalypse, many others. Introduction by Campbell Dodgson. 285pp. 8½ x 12¼.   21097-9 Pa. $6.00

THE DISASTERS OF WAR, Francisco Goya. 83 etchings record horrors of Napoleonic wars in Spain and war in general. Reprint of 1st edition, plus 3 additional plates. Introduction by Philip Hofer. 97pp. 9⅜ x 8¼.   21872-4 Pa. $3.00

ENGRAVINGS OF HOGARTH, William Hogarth. 101 of Hogarth's greatest works: Rake's Progress, Harlot's Progress, Illustrations for Hudibras, Midnight Modern Conversation, Before and After, Beer Street and Gin Lane, many more. Full commentary. 256pp. 11 x 14.   22479-1 Pa. $7.00
23023-6 Clothbd. $13.50

PRIMITIVE ART, Franz Boas. Great anthropologist on ceramics, textiles, wood, stone, metal, etc.; patterns, technology, symbols, styles. All areas, but fullest on Northwest Coast Indians. 350 illustrations. 378pp.   20025-6 Pa. $3.75

EGYPTIAN MAGIC, E.A. Wallis Budge. Foremost Egyptologist, curator at British Museum, on charms, curses, amulets, doll magic, transformations, control of demons, deific appearances, feats of great magicians. Many texts cited. 19 illustrations. 234pp.   USO 22681-6 Pa. $2.50

THE LEYDEN PAPYRUS: AN EGYPTIAN MAGICAL BOOK, edited by F. Ll. Griffith, Herbert Thompson. Egyptian sorcerer's manual contains scores of spells: sex magic of various sorts, occult information, evoking visions, removing evil magic, etc. Transliteration faces translation. 207pp.   22994-7 Pa. $2.50

THE MALLEUS MALEFICARUM OF KRAMER AND SPRENGER, translated, edited by Montague Summers. Full text of most important witchhunter's "Bible," used by both Catholics and Protestants. Theory of witches, manifestations, remedies, etc. Indispensable to serious student. 278pp. 6⅝ x 10.   USO 22802-9 Pa. $3.95

LOST CONTINENTS, L. Sprague de Camp. Great science-fiction author, finest, fullest study: Atlantis, Lemuria, Mu, Hyperborea, etc. Lost Tribes, Irish in pre-Columbian America, root races; in history, literature, art, occultism. Necessary to everyone concerned with theme. 17 illustrations. 348pp.   22668-9 Pa. $3.50

THE COMPLETE BO   OF CHARLES FORT, Charles Fort. Book of the Damned, Lo!, Wild Talents, New Lands. Greatest compilation of data: celestial appearances, flying saucers, falls of frogs, strange disappearances, inexplicable data not recognized by science. Inexhaustible, painstakingly documented. Do not confuse with modern charlatanry. Introduction by Damon Knight. Total of 1126pp.
                                                                  23094-5 Clothbd. $15.00

FADS AND FALLACIES IN THE NAME OF SCIENCE, Martin Gardner. Fair, witty appraisal of cranks and quacks of science: Atlantis, Lemuria, flat earth, Velikovsky, orgone energy, Bridey Murphy, medical fads, etc. 373pp.   20394-8 Pa. $3.50

HOAXES, Curtis D. MacDougall. Unbelievably rich account of great hoaxes: Locke's moon hoax, Shakespearean forgeries, Loch Ness monster, Disumbrationist school of art, dozens more; also psychology of hoaxing. 54 illustrations. 338pp.   20465-0 Pa. $3.50

THE GENTLE ART OF MAKING ENEMIES, James A.M. Whistler. Greatest wit of his day deflates Wilde, Ruskin, Swinburne; strikes back at inane critics, exhibitions. Highly readable classic of impressionist revolution by great painter. Introduction by Alfred Werner. 334pp.   21875-9 Pa. $4.00

THE BOOK OF TEA, Kakuzo Okakura. Minor classic of the Orient: entertaining, charming explanation, interpretation of traditional Japanese culture in terms of tea ceremony. Edited by E.F. Bleiler. Total of 94pp.   20070-1 Pa. $1.25